RECESS
BATTLES

RECESS BATTLES

Playing, Fighting, and Storytelling

Anna R. Beresin

Foreword by Brian Sutton-Smith

UNIVERSITY PRESS OF MISSISSIPPI / JACKSON

www.upress.state.ms.us

The University Press of Mississippi is a member of the
Association of American University Presses.

Artwork provided by the children of the Mill School.

First printing 2010
∞
Library of Congress Cataloging-in-Publication Data

Beresin, Anna R.
  Recess battles : playing, fighting, and storytelling / Anna R. Beresin ;
foreword by Brian Sutton-Smith.
      p. cm.
  Includes bibliographical references and index.
    ISBN 978-1-60473-739-4 (cloth : alk. paper) — ISBN 978-1-60473-740-0 (ebook)
  1. Recesses. 2. Play—United States. 3. Child development. I. Title.
  LB3033.B49 2010
  371.2'42—dc22   2010015104

British Library Cataloging-in-Publication Data available

To Noah, Matti, and Gabe, who have grown up with this book

CONTENTS

APPENDIXES

FOREWORD

BRIAN SUTTON-SMITH, Scholar in Residence, Strong National Museum of Play

Anna Beresin's analysis of the play life of children on the playground is a bit like reading about the Marxist revolution or even more powerfully about seeing the proletariat fighting for its rights while being slaughtered by the governing classes. In my thirty years as a university doctoral supervisor in psychology, education, and folklore, I have seldom if ever seen such a massive collection of data regarding what children are trying to do for themselves as human beings within their playgrounds and how teachers and other authorities are trying to interfere in the process.

This book is an earthshaking anthropology of the injustices being done to children by the abolition of recess, particularly among disadvantaged economic and racial school populations. It is also an implicit critique of the current idealization and rationalization of individual child development, as if any such located sociology is not relevant. Psychology's general focus on the idealization of children's solitary Kantian imagination is implicitly focused on individual children in their solitary playrooms with their solitary computers and personal television sets. The model is that of desk work in the middle-class work world.

But what is rewarding in this book about a modern nightmare is the account of the many ways in which these children nevertheless make a mockery of the school's and academic world's requirements by making up "abnormative" play forms within which physical skills, rhymes, and songs are rewarded. These forms of play, which authorities often try to ban, are often the only way in which these children come to terms with their confined school lives. They love to explain how well they can manage the game of wall ball or sing to stepping songs that challenge adult prudery. Here you find the only place where they can harbor a real pride in their own accomplishments. Thank you, Anna.

ACKNOWLEDGMENTS

I began this research project carrying my one-year-old on my back: he now shaves, giving new meaning to the phrase *longitudinal study*. Along the way, many people have carried this project with me, providing support, humor, and encouragement for an offbeat, play-inspired major work. I am grateful to the University Press of Mississippi for taking on such an unusual multidisciplinary topic.

Initially supported by a Spencer Grant and a Mellon Award, the project blossomed at the University of Pennsylvania. A great player of ideas, Brian Sutton-Smith both challenged and encouraged this project. To him and to his colleagues, Roger Abrahams, Dan Ben-Amos, Frederick Erickson, Kenny Goldstein, Adam Kendon, and Robert Blair St. George, I offer my gratitude for their flexibility.

The University of the Arts supplied several faculty grants for digital equipment and art supplies that literally frame this study. My colleagues and my playful art students model many of the ideas in this book—the play of ideas is a serious art, and no one ever said it had to be boring.

I owe my first formal training in child observation to David Elkind at Tufts University, who along with the playground designer Anita Rui Olds challenged me to see the complex beauty of children's play. Milton Chen, Carol Gilligan, Donald Oliver, and David Perkins of the Harvard Graduate School of Education showed me how to observe without romanticism. But the first expert I ever encountered is still my favorite: my mother, Marjorie Richman, a board member of the Child Center of New York and an earnest advocate for poor minority children, a great teller of stories. Thanks to my dad, Seymour Richman, promoter of all things technical, for his multimedia advice and encouragement. A sweeping, dramatic low bow to you both.

I have been blessed with steady technical hands, attached to the bodies of Mira Adornetto, Larry Cohen, Eileen Flanagan, Pritha Gopalen, Debby Pollack, Joey Raicovich, and Erin Slonaker. In this multimedia world, no one can do it alone. Thanks to Purdue University Press and Myrdene Anderson for allowing bits to be reprinted from the fine volume *The Cultural Shaping of Violence* and to Libby Tucker of the *Children's Folklore Review* for allowing part of "Sui Generis" to be reprinted. Thanks also to Taylor and Francis for permission to excerpt from *Children's Folklore: A Sourcebook.*

When I desperately needed writing feedback, friends, family members, and colleagues offered good cheer and specific suggestions: Jerry Allender, Carl and Connie Beresin, Gabe Beresin, Matti Beresin, Noah Beresin, David Bromley, Mindy Brown, Rory Cohen, Wendy Epstein, Eileen Flanagan, Fran Fox, Nancy Heller, Susan Landau, Mara Natkins, Barb and Charlie Richman, Libby Smith, Bob Zatzman, and Heather Zimmerman. Anonymous reviewer Dan Cook did the bravest thing of all, unmasking himself to offer encouragement and networking. May you all have such critics that become friends.

No one has listened more than my husband, Neil, with wise editing, basketball advice, and countless 2:00 A.M. queries about whether this was indeed the best-sounding title. You alone have shown me how words cannot express the deepest emotions, though play and love can. No one has given more than the teachers of the Mill School, who do the nearly impossible task of educating children in an underfunded and overcrowded environment. No one has opened their hearts to me more in this project than the children of the Mill School. I wish I could thank you all by your real names, but then again, I promised. To Ms. Wembley, who cried with me over the struggles of urban education; and to Tashi, who sang loudest; and to Tommy, who gave me his last, red, sour Crybaby: Thanks.

RECESS
BATTLES

INTRODUCTION

Tensions in an Urban American School Yard

Nike, Nike,	Eedie Idie Odie
Who can do	Here Comes the Teacher
the Nike?	with a Big Fat Stick
Foot to the	Now it's time for
N-I-K-E	'Rhythmatic
And hop to the	One and one, two
N-I-K-E	Two and two, four
And bounce to the	Now it's time for
N-I-K-E	Spelling
And criss to the	What's C-A-T? Cat!
N-I-K-E	And R-A-T? Rat!
And turn to the	Now it's time for
N-I-K-E	History

The Mill School Yard, Philadelphia, Pennsylvania, 2004

Classic signs of an active children's culture are all over the Mill School yard.[1] Chalk games are not allowed, but painted graffiti ebbs and flows like waves on the freshly repainted school walls. Shoes dangle from the telephone wires above the iron fence. Balls bounce off walls, rocks are thrown onto hopscotches, and singing games can be heard above the din of laughter and screaming. Every nook and cranny of this school yard is used for some kind of play, from the lone tree that becomes a base for chasing games to the sand from the graffiti-removing power wash—voices, hands, and feet in motion.

On the first day of school, September 1991, I was apologetically told that yard time had officially been canceled that year because of school yard violence. The Mill School, a pseudonym for a working-class, multiracial public elementary school, sits on a busy truck route in a part of Philadelphia known for its deep union affiliations and its history of racism. I had come to record the children's games and interview this unusually diverse collection of children about their folklore. At 10:30 in the morning, I noticed that children were indeed filing outside for recess, contrary to the principal's plan. He turned to one of the sixth-grade teachers, kindly Ms. Wembley, and asked whether or not the students were to have recess. She explained that it was the only time she could go to the bathroom each morning. Thanks to her bladder, five hundred children were allowed to have morning play.

In reality, Ms. Wembley used the fifteen minutes of school yard time for a whole day's worth of phone calls, catching up with parents of students in trouble, accommodating needy children, lobbying for much-needed supplies, and even grading papers. The children were pleased with the default policy that allowed them to play; officially allotted twenty minutes, recess was usually closer to fifteen and often disappeared altogether if trouble broke out. From 1991 to 2004, recess disappeared, reappeared as gym, disappeared again, reappeared as a consequence of teachers' demands for their own break, reemerged as part of a formal-sounding "Socialized Recess" program, and then was removed from the morning and added to lunch.

With school resources dwindling and increased pressure to teach for testing success, the reduction in recess is seen as a way simultaneously to increase "order" and instructional time. It is seen as an efficiency issue. During the years of no recess, the students were more "under control," according to the principal, but his secretary commented that the kindergarteners were wetting themselves because they could not wait until lunch for a break. Ironically, recess was removed at the same time that American children were beginning to be heavily medicated for hyperactivity and an inability to sit still.[2] When recess was denied to the fourth- and fifth-graders in 1993, I was told that the time was needed by the school and that nine-, ten-, and eleven-year-old children were considered "too old to play."

In Philadelphia, teachers are required to have breaks and are backed by the union, but the children lack this support. Gym is required for children's physical health, but even children know the difference between recess and gym.

First of all, we get a grade in gym.
And it's hot in there.
Yeah, it's hot.
And sometimes we have to do what the teacher says.
Outside we can just run free.

The students not only can run free outside but also are allowed to speak and move in a manner that does not require adult approval. Outside, stories and games emerge, providing a detailed and absurd cultural commentary. These commentaries, stylized by rich ethnic traditions, help mediate the worlds of childhood and the worlds of grown-ups. Like the classics of play therapy, which illuminate the inner workings of individual children's minds, the school yard shouts cultural texts—the inner workings of sets of children's minds as they negotiate their cultural worlds.[3] From "N-I-K-E" to Silent Numbers to Suicide Handball, those stories and games illustrate the battles for and in recess in this one school yard at the turn of the millennium.

All of the ideas in this book were initiated by conversations with the children. Ten months of daily fieldwork in 1991 were followed by three months of fieldwork in 1999 and more in 2004. Eight-, nine-, ten-, and eleven-year-old children were observed, interviewed in small groups, audiotaped, and eventually videotaped. These videotapes were replayed to the children and their teachers for commentary and were then coded and analyzed for patterning. More than two hundred children participated actively in the study, while close to fifteen hundred children were observed. The children guided me to pay attention to the small things, to appreciate their skills and "the human seriousness of play."[4]

This book frames the children's worlds with the voices of the grown-ups whose power literally surrounds these children. Commentary by the adult staff suggests a widespread misreading of the complexities of school yard play and its social, emotional, intellectual, physical, and cultural utility. Part 1, "Playin' and Fighting," demonstrates through video microethnographic evidence that this school yard's play is not violent, although the grown-ups at the Mill School are convinced that it is. Spontaneous storytelling with violent themes is presented to demonstrate how children integrate images of larger cultural battles within their creative peer culture. Games emerge as alternative form of storytelling, a process I call gametelling, and guide us through passion for performance and through frequency.[5] The book juggles not only texts, video transcripts, and commentaries but also game popularity and frequency as markers of cultural significance.

Part 2, "The Push and Pull of Adult Culture," describes the tensions between larger cultural forces and the power of the institution of school. We see the dramatic rise of commercially scripted singing games. Sometimes the game serves as a subtle form of children's cultural commentary; sometimes it screams that commentary right at you. Always it reflects the realities and absurdities of the children's larger world, serving as both "model and mirror" of larger cultural values.[6] The grown-ups attempt to edit what is played and what is not played, with varying success and many costs. The larger tension surrounding restricted movement in a scripted world presents new ways of looking at children's socialization.

Part 3, "Play and Children's Culture," addresses the complex literature about play and offers suggestions to those concerned about children's right to play. A most mysterious and complicated form of communication, play has much to tell us about how culture is edited and created anew.

The book focuses on this triangle of scripting, bodily freedom, and adult control, arguing that these two developments—an increase in commercially sponsored play and a decrease in playtime and freedom of movement—present an interesting and troubling dialectic in the school yard, troubling in its manifestation of children's stress and its adult misperceptions. Children are desperate to play, struggling in the art of cultural adaptation in a framework that is itself resistant to change. Yet there is exuberance.

Each chapter is introduced by a painting created by one of the third-graders of 2004. Many had never before used a paintbrush, and the occasion marked the first time they had access to as much drawing paper as they wished. "Yes, Yes, No Rematch, Bring It On!" cries one painting. Look for the ecstatic ballplayers, the anticipatory basketball shot, and the sunshine spreading over a turning jump rope. Next to a hopscotch, one drawing simply states, "I am happy." This book, its paintings, and its recordings are presented not only to tell the stories of the school yard but also to attempt to capture how those stories were told and what was said most. Games embody a heroic struggle; the children manage to say so much to each other and to us in just fifteen minutes a day.

There are many ways to introduce these stories, and I confess that I have played with many of them. Chronology, theory, and a summary of similar monographs offer useful starting places, but I prefer to have the main characters introduce their viewpoints. In addition to Ms. Wembley, the accidental setter of policy, I present ten-year-old Joey, ten-year-old Tashi, and Mr. Mann, the security guard who oversees the playground with his team of nonteaching aides. We begin with these and other voices of the school yard and move to theory and academic knowledge. Like other ethnographers, I give them equal weight.

Joey, a pale boy with spiky light brown hair, came up with the title for part 1: Recess? "It's about playin' and fightin'." Tashi, a brown-skinned girl with doe eyes and a toothy smile, inspired part 2. "Nike, Nike, Who Can Do the Nike?" and "Eedie, Idie, Odie, Here Comes the Teacher with the Big Fat Stick" are the easiest jump rope games to learn, she told me. Her ten-year-old girlfriends agreed, nodding their braided heads as they stood on the concrete slab that is their school yard. But these games really were no easier than many others in their repertoire, and I realized that the games' popularity, frequency, and ordering are actually clues—arrows that the children have been using to point toward the central struggles of their childhoods. These rhymes represent commercialization and the children's physical struggle for autonomy within the controlling realm of school. This realization prompted me look for contrasts, dialectics, ironies.

Tashi was skipping, dragging the short plastic rope that the school provided, when I first met her. She and her friends were not jumping at the time; the only rope they had was much too short, and the school did not provide enough long ones. The girls walked around under the basketball space that had no hoop and that was decorated only with a sticker reading, "Basketball—The Antidrug." Children were told to play but not run. To play games but use no supplies. To think for themselves but conform and not talk back. They were lucky, though—their older classmates had experienced the repeated cancellation of recess, its reinstatement, and its rearrangement as a brief outside break at the end of lunch. After fifteen minutes of outside time, the bell rang, and the teachers and teaching assistants chased the children not with actual big fat sticks but with whistles and threats of punishment. Playtime was officially over, and the children sang to themselves as they ambled back to their classrooms.

Underneath these larger battles lie other interesting tensions, dramas that have changed in their intensity over time: racial tensions, tensions among social classes, and tensions between boys and girls. Over the thirteen-year span of this study, games that were strictly African American were learned by European Americans, and boys' games were gradually learned by girls. Racial desegregation gave way to economic desegregation when the school changed its status from a desegregated magnet school to a No Child Left Behind school.[7] When the study began, the school was evenly racially integrated, but over time it has moved to an African American majority. Consistent from the early 1990s to the early 2000s was the school's overall distrust of children's culture, its messages, and its utility. The most significant tension lies in the children's need to express cultural confusion and the adult agenda to subdue play—if necessary, by force.

Mr. Mann, a middle-aged retired police officer employed as a security guard, was often hassled by students whose names he did not know. Mr. Mann spoke most often about the control of play:

> You can't be nice. Especially. You have to be nasty. The kids have nightmares about me. They won't come to school. [Smiles] They cry. [One aide] is nasty. [Another aide is] abusive. She grabs them up. I don't do that anymore. Man who trains 'em says they can't do that. After a while, they won't respect you. It's psychology. It's a mind game. That's the only way you can control people, by your mind. And the parents are crazy.
>
> From now on I'm not talking to [one particular boy] anymore. I might warn him one time, but I might not. He can figure it out; he won't even know what he did wrong. He's supposed to know what the rules are. I just point; I don't have to warn him, and . . . I don't think I am. [Points to the boy] He's crazy.

The removal of playtime was often used as a punishment. In 1999, there were often whole classes standing "against the wall," missing recess for one reason or another.[8] When the bell rang and the children gathered into lines, an aide hollered,

> Two lines, or you're staying in for next recess. You know what, Room 2? We'll make it the rest of the week as soon as your teacher comes out, since you all got an itch in your throats.

Everyone—teachers *and* children—agrees that inside recess is the worst. When it is raining, the children eat and then go sit in the auditorium. Here, the removal of play is used as a convenience—a way to maintain control. The air is punitive:

> I allow you to talk, you are allowed to talk. But you don't know how to talk. No, I will separate you if I hear anything. That means no talking. I said be quiet. Sit right there. I don't want to answer any questions. You're supposed to be sitting there. I told you you could talk, but you don't know how to talk nicely and quietly. We're gonna call your mother and see if your mother wants you to rap in school. If that's the case, then we'll have you up on stage. Keep your hands off each other. Sit down back there, young man.

The lunch lady, Miss Jones, is the softest on the children. She has an "if I don't see it, it is okay" policy on both rainy and sunny days.

> They go straight out and play basketball. . . . They don't eat, they just go straight out. . . . They're not allowed to eat or drink out there. Don't put it in my face—I won't see it. Don't get caught.

The children choose to play rather than eat, risk being yelled at to express themselves, and are encouraged to sneak out to get their needs met. School is a tense place for both the children and the grown-ups, and the children suffer to communicate what is inside them. The kinder teachers and the softer aides compensate by sidestepping small rules, just like the children do. Older children—ten, eleven, and twelve—"don't need to play," but they sneak out to do so; their lunch period is considered "worse than" that of the eight- and nine-year-olds, and the staff believe that the older the child, the worse the child behaves.

This book does not examine the making of policy or the educational uses of games, although I believe that games have a tremendously useful educational potential. Rather, this book documents what children do with play as expressive culture while they learn to function in their society. Children in hunting cultures play with toy bows and arrows, and children in digging cultures practice digging. The Mill School children toy with the messages of their larger world. These children make the overwhelming power of adults tolerable through the alternative track of bodily expression. Their bodies offer a way of taking in culture and rearranging it, taking it apart without taking it in whole. Yet their bodies are increasingly controlled by the school. To examine one process without examining the other does a disservice to the complexity of childhood. Given the extreme misunderstanding of the significance of play, one could say that children are in fact facing a crisis of their own cultural expression.

As singing games and sports become more scripted, children's bodies draw on other scripts, borrowing them if necessary from old school game traditions. Steps, numbers, and older singing games celebrate the body, while handball and mock violent play test its limits. Sports become studies of invention, and folk games slide into professionalism. The school yard emerges as a cultural window, reflective and open, showing life that is no more chaotic than our larger culture but perhaps showing it to us more clearly. In short, while the school yard is being squeezed, the children, just like their teachers, find creative ways to wring the most out of their limited resources. But children who do not have the freedom to move incur costs—depression, aggression, and apathy.

Although many books have examined schools' curtailment of game play, gender variation, ethnic difference,[9] or the influence of advertising on schools in general,[10] this work is the first to examine the intersection of these phenomena and its relationship to children's experiences. Most psychological studies of play[11] see children's inventions as individual productions, while anthropological collections[12] see the play of children outside the West as products of culture. This book is distinguished by its documentation of children's culturally stylized processes of invention within the framework of a particular urban historical context. The children creatively linked competing arguments together throughout their songs and games, and they are in fine academic company.

Cultural analyst Paul Willis writes of the strange relationship between consumption and work, "Whereas the ideal model for the worker is the good time kept, the disciplined and empty head, the model for the consumer is the converse—a head full of unbounded appetites for symbolic things."[13] The working-class work environment represses choice, while consumer culture explodes it. The same tension is visible in this working-class school: The school represses motion and expression, while the commercial world of advertisements pulls the children into a cornucopia of desire. How does the child manage to be both empty and full of images, a controlled body with different scripts vying for memorization? How has school become a place of empty-headedness, while advertisements, mindless in their simplistic repetition, now represent knowledge? Unlike other cultural analysts,[14] Willis is both critical and optimistic: "There is a strange unanimity—and ghostly embrace of the opposites—between left and right when it comes to a condemnation of consumerism and especially of the penetration of the market into cultural matters. . . . We disagree with both assessments, especially their shared underlying pessimism. They both ignore the dynamic and living qualities of everyday culture and especially their necessary work and symbolic creativity. . . . Cultural commodities are catalysts, not product; a stage in, not the destination of, cultural affairs."[15]

But commodities are only a useful cultural catalyst if children have the freedom to turn them into something useful or have the skill to do so without official permission. Otherwise, the commercials merely become scripts for the working-class children to practice their roles as potential consumers and future holders of minimum-wage jobs.[16]

Psychologist Brian Sutton-Smith has written much about the "ambiguity of play," referring to an ambiguity not only in the mixing of larger cultural messages but also in the tentative messages to the players.[17] His ideas of "the dialectic of games" and "games as a model of power" are instrumental. Willis and Sutton-Smith serve as my theoretical home base and point to the utility of a multidisciplinary approach that is both ethnographic and wide-angled.

The school yard is an ideal bounded framework for psychological and cultural study, as Margaret Mead told her students.[18] The school yard is limited in time and space and contains the same diversity of players day in and day out. The activity is as open-ended and as consistent as one can find in a child's social world, yet it remains a virtually untapped scholarly resource, in part because of the vastness of its frame and in part because it possesses a complexity that requires the perspectives of more than one discipline.

The linking of psychological and cultural patterning has its philosophic roots in both the Culture and Personality School and the Frankfurt School of sociology.[19] The former emphasized cultural variation and human development; the latter sought to link Freudian theory with Marxist theory. Both groups had scholars who focused on power relationships and expressive culture, most notably Culture and Personality's Gregory Bateson and Frankfurt's Walter Benjamin.[20] For Bateson, scholars were microanalysts and recorders of paradoxes; the study of play was primarily concerned with the ambiguity of communication in a bounded framework. For Benjamin, scholars were to serve as the voice of criticism, protectors of children's art forms in particularly hostile historical contexts. For both Bateson and Benjamin, the study of style was by definition a contextualized process, and different contexts required more than one box of scholarly tools.

Like his contemporary Erik Erikson, Bateson was fascinated by the double binds of culture, and both of these theorists were powerfully drawn to play.[21] When a system embraces opposite mandates, those without power are placed in the position of making sense as best they can, sometimes choosing depression, aggression, or furtive creativity. Bateson, a pioneer, along with Mead, in the use of film as a documentary tool, pushes us to see frame and play simultaneously, teasing apart cultural norms and viewing them from different perspectives. Video analysts such as Ray Birdwhistell, Frederick Erickson, and Adam Kendon have built on this foundation to both microanalyze and quantify the patterns of human interaction.[22] Beginning with the audio or video document, we can count frequency, check reliability, and test assumptions by presenting the raw material to a variety of players. Through video and audio recording, we gain a form of witnessing, and through its analysis we have a way of shedding light both externally and from within.[23]

Multidisciplinary scholars, themselves rooted in Frankfurt School ideology, including Michel Foucault and Pierre Bourdieu, have emphasized the interactions that occurs among people, their time in history, their creations, and the institutional frameworks that in some way shape those lives and creations. Although much has been written about the institutional framework of schooling in the lives of children, especially with a Foucauldian or Bourdieusian lens,[24] little attention has been paid to the complexities of play in an institutional setting and even less to the socialization of working-class multiethnic groups.[25] In essence, I borrow those lenses and apply a different set of tools to a different set of problems.

Folklorists, who win the title of having taken children's games most seriously, have often left their collections in midair, presenting interesting romanticized poems with little attention to context. The exceptions are scholars of history, such as folklorists Iona and Peter Opie,[26] the great collectors of British games, and Sutton-Smith,[27] their rival in the study of the games of New Zealand and the Americas. Onwuchekwa Jemie, scholar of African and African American play, has recently published a great addition to the American canon.[28] Like the Opies and Sutton-Smith, Jemie recognizes the twists and turns of history and presents the children's games as witty alternative historical commentaries that are tangible, skillful, and sometimes shocking.[29] Like anthropologist Helen Schwartzman, psychologist Rivka Eifermann, and sociologist Barre Thorne, these collectors of games seek to embed game study in the larger time and place, a reflection of culture and the habits of the mind.[30] As developmentalist Jean Piaget has brilliantly noted, games offer an entranceway into the social worlds of children, requiring the analysis of the genres that children prefer above any other: "Children's games constitute the most admirable of social institutions."[31] My analysis draws heavily on his contributions, expanding to a cultural lens of the contributions of play. As the games are complex, the theoretical and methodological toolbox is quite large.

Before policies are changed—indeed, before recess is removed altogether—it behooves us to see what actually occurs in the school yard. For many children from culturally or economically homogenous neighborhoods, yard time offers the only chance to play with children of different ethnic or socioeconomic backgrounds. The school yard is a laboratory of socialization, both for students and for scholars, because the children holler to one another what is on their minds.

The same Ms. Wembley who okayed recess in 1991 was popping extra-strength pain relievers when I returned in 1999. She spoke of her worries about specific children. One sixth-grader lives in a homeless shelter; her mother is gone, and the child and her sister have been placed with two different agencies. Ms. Wembley thinks recess is "cute" but is more worried about the kids who cannot read, function, or get jobs. Teen pregnancy is up. For her, the function of elementary school is reduced to teaching children to read and to avoid pregnancy. The school was lucky to have her; she cared so deeply. But school, like play, has many functions, and they relate complexly in a complicated world. Random policies that remove and reinstate recess are doubly damaging in violent times. By 2004, both Ms. Wembley and Mr. Mann were gone, transferred to other schools.

Outside in the school yard, Tashi's eyes grew wide when I asked if in 2004 the children still sing "Big Mac," the most popular jump rope song in 1991 and 1999. "You know 'Big Mac'?" she asked. She began to sing, "Big Mac, Filet o' Fish, Quarter Pounder," and I sang along with her, "Frenchie fries, icee Coke, milk shake foot," watching her eyes growing to comical proportions. She was like an expatriate who discovers that someone else speaks her mother tongue. When the children realized I admired what they admired—game cleverness, physical skill, irony, and humor—they often offered me a jump. I explained that I was there to watch them play and listen to what they liked to sing. "Oh," offered Trudy, "you study what we kids do." This is as succinct an introduction as any other.

Ace, Ace No Higher.

- Part 1 -

PLAYIN' AND FIGHTIN'

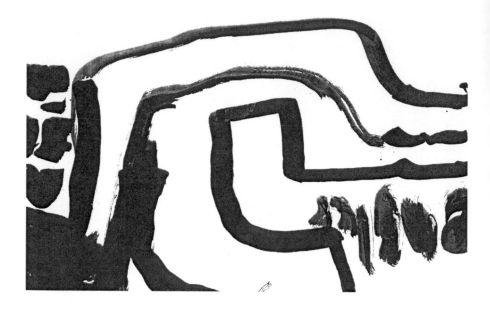

- 1 -

VIOLENCE AS "THE RECESS PROBLEM"

Mr. Rumble, an energetic, middle-aged white man, wore professional clothes and sparkled with the energy of someone who was confident in his role as principal. He welcomed me as a fellow professional and became nostalgic for his graduate school days. A man in transition, he allowed me complete access to the school for research purposes. I observed not only the school yard but the cafeteria, the gym, the evening holiday performances, and the third-, fourth-, fifth-, and sixth-grade classrooms, and hung out in the teachers' lounge. Eventually I was allowed to videotape—with parental permission—from the school's second-floor window and on the playground itself.

As part of my agreement with Mr. Rumble, I was asked to find patterns of aggression in the school yard as I recorded the children's folk games. This agreement rationalized my constant presence, given the ever-present concerns regarding "school yard violence" and "the recess problem." Because educators assumed that recess was violent, playtime had been canceled, reintroduced, canceled again, turned into gym, made into a formalized program, and then reinstituted as a consequence of teachers' union demands. Years after the first cancellation, teachers at the school still spoke of "the recess problem," and I set out to find out what that problem was.

In the teachers' lounge and in university libraries, the playground has typically been associated with violence, chaos, and bullying rather than what I saw: friendship, skill, challenge, and the negotiation of culture. The grown-ups of the Mill School consistently used *chaotic, wild*, and *unruly* to describe school yard happenings. Their eyes saw the zigzagging runners and the children who refused to cooperate to line up and were surprised that the children actually played as many games as they did.

The staff grimaced at games with names that invoked mock violence (Suicide Handball and the Fighting Game) yet were nostalgic about their own childhood games, which they remembered with difficulty (Red Rover, tag, dodgeball). Educators used the violent game titles to rationalize militancy and told stories of children needing to be taken to the nurse after recess play. Given the Mill School's mix of pretend violent drama and real aggression, distinctions used by animal ethologists to study play fighting in the wild offer the most useful place to start.

Gregory Bateson, ever watchful of animal play, notes that play fighting is very much like the real thing but is not the real thing exactly.[1] Play fighting and real aggression are communicatively different, signaling different kinds of relationships, even though the mock and the real fighting can slip from one to another in an instant. In play fighting, the children, like animals, generally remain together after the episode is over. In moments of real fighting, the individuals separate.[2] The quality of the activity is signaled by this extension of continued relationship or the breaking up of the interaction.

Anthony Pellegrini's work on rough-and-tumble play has raised some important questions regarding the exact descriptions of this type of activity, highlighting adult misperceptions about what is destructive and what is merely playful.[3] But the literature on play fighting has virtually ignored children's control or lack of control in the creation of violent moments. I decided to have the children give advice about "the recess problem" and to comb through the video ethnographic data to look for patterns. Where and when were children getting hurt in the school yard? Is the removal of their playtime justified, or is it, as sociologist Pierre Bourdieu would suggest, a "useful fiction"?[4]

In their interviews, the children gave clues to the key moments to be studied. They repeatedly mentioned the difficulty of ending recess and how children were often hurt while lining up. One boy who spoke little during our discussions said that "going in was the worst part of school." It was the pointer I was looking for.

When the bell rings, we like—
When the bell rings—
We try to stay there—
I know!
When the bell rings, and when our teacher [speaking urgently into the microphone]—
When the bell rings and when our teacher, and when they don't come, and when they don't come out early—
Yeah.
We start playing rope again!
And when the bell rings I like to pick on—I like to hit the boys [excited chatter].
We like to hit them upside the head, and then they're always chasing after us, but we run.
Some people go and line up—some people go and line up and fight in line.
Some people run around in the back of the line.
People pull hair.
Yeah.
And let their hair get all messed up.
They do steps in back of the line.
And because they just pulled their hair or something like that.
Yeah, like my hair—see how it's all messed up?
And they clown around or something.
They don't like them, they start fighting.

The clues were: "When the bell rings"; "I like to hit the boys, go in line . . . and fight in line"; "Going in is the worst part of school." I asked in small-group interviews about what happens when the bell rings.

We get mad.
(You get mad?)
Sometimes Ms. Gee keeps us for recess, and that's not fair.
But a lot of times they be cuttin' us out, they be cuttin' us out on the bell, because sometimes they just be like, 10:20 and they ring the bell.

In addition to the games, I filmed the lining-up procedure and the school yard in its entirety in wide angle. I then coded all incidents of violence, no matter how trivial, as either mock violence, where the players stayed together, or serious aggression, where the players separated. An interesting pattern emerged.

WIDE-ANGLE FOOTAGE

In the wide-angle footage, I looked for violence and noted its type and timing. Because I used two different cameras, some times are listed by hour:minute:seconds (e.g., 10:44:21), while some are listed according to minutes and seconds by a counter (25:34). The relation of the timing of the action to the sound of the bell, not the absolute time, is what is significant.

The hour:minute:second footage was taken from a second-floor window and was focused on the interaction while students were in line. Although the minute:second footage lacked this focus, the tapes of recess in June had a line closer to the building than the early fall footage taken with the same camera. As a result, a general wider angle was able to capture basic gestures and facial features, which are necessary for this type of coding.[5] This analysis includes all relevant footage taken that was in focus during the 1991–92 school year. To have two cameras going simultaneously, one at the window, and one in the school yard, I worked with a trusty assistant.

Eight of these nine days showed distinct violence in the lining-up procedure, with six of the incidents occurring less than one minute from the ringing of the bell and the other two occurring within two minutes of the bell. Only two instances visible in all the wide-angle footage occurred at a time other than at the transition period. Some of the conflict that was not related to lining up occurred right at the beginning of recess, during another transition.

Anthropologists, psychologists, and sociologists have long written about transition times and spaces as wrought with danger and the possibility of creativity.[6] Rites of passage focus on transitions in time; amulets and decorations guard transitional windows and doors in many traditional cultures. Tollbooths are known as zones of accidents, and many an

Date	Description	Time of Act	Time of Bell
11/4	a) Real fighting—pushing, kicking in back of line, leads to ripple effect of stylized violence	10:44:21	
	b) More real fighting, escalated; they separate, withdraw face gaze	10:44:35	10:42:38
11/8	No incidents		
11/15	a) Real fighting—slugging; it continues, they leave each other	10:41:56	
	b) Much wrestling in line		
	c) Fight in line, visible anger	10:44:18	10:42:26
11/18	a) Three rounds of mock but direct fighting at beginning of recess; third round is real fight, broken up by older girl	10:30:04 10:30:42 10:31:02	
	b) Brawl with crowd, ended by aide	10:31:50	
	c) Fight—student thrown to ground, retaliation	10:42:48	10:42:24
	d) Girl hits a child in line as retaliation	10:44:22	
11/25	a) Boy is pushed to ground, kicked, actors stay together	10:32:48	
	b) Fight begins	10:41:42	10:42:44
	c) Fourth-grader pushes everyone in his line	10:43:53	
	d) Girls punch and kick in retaliation		
6/1	a) Play fighting in line joined by another boy who is less playful and then is seriously pushed in annoyance by one of the initial participants	25:34	24:37
6/2	a) As line is about to go in, fourth-grader turns to hit third-grader: bullying stance, another third-grader intervenes; a teacher then stops the incident	21:49	20:17
6/3	a) Fight starts, two on one, victim stalks back, later they separate	21:47	20:59
6/4	a) Second person in third-grade line grabs person in front of him, who throws him to the ground; grabber is hurt in the process. Ripple effect in pushing	34:14	33:46
	b) Kicking, pushing, banging—two boys test the boundaries away from the line	34:18	
	c) In line, tagging becomes hitting, then retaliation as students are thrown to the ground. Chain reaction to four couples, male and female, sparring harshly	36:22	

argument occurs in the last few minutes of a visit with a friend or loved one. This phenomenon also appears in the school yard.

The ripple effect is visible in several of the tapes; pushing in line leads to retaliation, sometimes from bystanders, who then bump into other students. The sudden cessation of official games, the children's close proximity and high excitement levels, and a long period of waiting to go inside clearly set the stage for violent interaction.[7]

In these cases of real fighting, the children do not have to physically separate because they are technically not allowed to do so, and attempting to get away from each other would be to lose face in a potentially humiliating public arena. Instead, we must look for the removal of the gaze, reorientation of the body, and visible signs of anger, including the intensity and speed of the physical response. In line, the children seem to have more difficulty reading each other's clues—on two occasions, the two play fighters were joined in earnest by an outsider who then received serious retaliation from the initial play fighters.

ZOOM FOOTAGE

In these episodes, the camera was often focusing on a game and fighting emerged in or around the play activity. Again, note the timing of the bell.

In all but one of the zoom images, the fighting occurs within a minute and a half of the ringing of the bell. Violence is clearly part of the transition time and is otherwise rarely visible in the play period. The problem was not play itself but the in-between state between playtime and class time.

Some of the examples occurred within seconds of the bell. The violent talk had a wider window of about two or three minutes, but the violent aftershock of the bell was clearly visible even with this initial small sample. In these examples, only one serious play fight took place outside of the transition period. The last example shows a gap of more than three minutes, but although a long time had passed since the bell rang, the violence occurred only forty-seven seconds before the students walked back into the building. The transition may have two parts, given the children's extended waiting period.

Date	Description	Time of Act	Time of Bell
3/10	a) Play fighting sustained between boy and girl, slapping, pulling	10:37:64	
	b) Real punches/fight in line	10:42:16	10:42:00
3/20	a) Play fighting turned into a brawl; stopped by aide after bell	10:43:12	10:41:56
5/6	No incidents		
5/7	a) Immediately after bell, girl is pushed to ground, she cries	10:47:29	10:47:26
5/11	a) Two boys wrestle and part	10:45:28	10:44:25
	b) Girl approaches camera and announces, "Hello, I'm getting ready to beat this boy up right now. His name is Mark Jones, and he's—" Her friend interrupts, "She's going to beat him up"	10:47:31	
5/12	No incidents		
5/13	No incidents		
5/14	No incidents		
5/15	No incidents		
6/1	a) In back of line, fourth-grader kicks three third-graders	10:48:39	10:47:37
6/2	a) Play fight bordering on real fight with pushing	10:43:39	
	b) Teacher grabs jump rope, yanks it; children keep playing	10:50:03	10:49:00
	c) Play fighting turns into boxing in back of line; children separate	10:50:28	
6/3	a) Elaborate mock fight ("Beat him! Put him in the corner!"), but "victim" runs away ("Don't kill him") and dramatically crosses camera	10:40:42	10:48:00
6/4	No incidents		
6/22	a) "I socked him, I finally socked him," a child announces to camera	10:45:54	10:43:52
	b) Immigrant boy is on the floor, in tears, being pushed by another	10:47:11	
		(time of reentry to building: 10:47:58)	

Ironically, the teachers greet their students only during the transition period. When the teachers arrive, they witness the worst part of the students' behavior, and like the story of the blind men and the elephant, they assume the tail is equal to the whole thing. The nonteaching aides who see the entire experience range from good-natured to policing and aggressive, waiting for the few children to "act out" and "mess up," pink slips at the ready.

During the transition, attempts at authoritarian control worked only temporarily. A day after a severe talk by the principal was no different than the day before, even though the children considered him strict and powerful and were somewhat frightened of his authority. Even threats could not control the tremendous energy unleashed in the clashing of peer cultures with each other and with the institution of school.

"That ball is mine now." "You think you'll get it back?" "No playing." "No hopping." The teachers were not out yet, and the aides struggled to get the children to stop playing. As the games were officially over, it was a no-man's-land, and no one was in charge. The games, organizations of rhythm and motion, were stopped, and the four "recess ladies" and the armed security guard turned to threats and tough tones to calm down the children. The two hundred or so feet from the site of the lineup to the school doors felt like miles.

What is perceived as a recess problem here is in fact merely a transition problem. Yet the removal of play merely created other problems, tossing out the baby with the bathwater. Without recess, opportunities for creative expression, physical release, socialization, and the processing of complicated psychological, sociological, and cultural texts and images are lost. Without recess, the children lose art, relaxation, friendship, and the chance to collectively makes sense of the world around them. Given the children's passion for their games as forms of skill and expression, the fiction of recess as dangerous is a significant narrative of misdirected power.

When I shared the results of this study with the Mill School's new principal, Ms. Smith, in 1999, she was intrigued by the notion that recess "could be good for children." When asked, I offered that plenty of evidence shows that play is good for children and that when children do not play, it is a typically a sign of poor health. To her credit, when she heard about the transitional violence in her school yard, she sped up the transition process. Instead of waiting five or ten minutes with no one in charge and no teacher to claim them, the children were scooped up more quickly, and the lineup was moved nearer to the building.

Lots of changes have helped shift the violent dynamic at the Mill School. By 2004, the school had yet another principal, Ms. Jones, and a new security guard, Mr. Point, who seemed to know the children by name. More wraparound programs were in place for children in crisis. The lineup was even quicker, and the security guard mused that the school had become a "good school" compared with the one from which he transferred, where he had volunteered to walk children home after school so they would not get shot. "Good school" is now a designation of being less dangerous than a "bad school." Yet signs of drug dealing still littered the Mill School yard, and violence, although not as visible within the school's boundaries, was still mentioned in hushed tones, "up the avenue" and at the school down the block "where kids are really bad."

The cafeteria at lunch offered a taste of bedlam. There, like the class-room, much was given, little was taken in, and hardly anything or any-one was allowed to move or be moved. "It wasn't designed for so many bodies," said the building maintenance chief. The children knew that this statement was true, so while they waited to go outside, or on rainy days, or on days of punishment, their games became smaller or more subversive or disappeared.[8] I was worried about the children who were not playing, those sitting passively staring into space. Some of them went outside and remained this way, slumped against the wall, immo-bile, invisible to staff more worried about transgressors. The sneaky ones, the ones who kept playing, who whispered cheers and stories as they lined up, who bounced their handballs until they got to the door—they were the ones to follow.

- 2 -

STORYTELLING AND CHILDREN'S BATTLES

The children soon realized that they were allowed to say anything in my presence. The fourth-grade boys particularly enjoyed saying curse words and uncensored versions of popular raps into my microphone. Aisha, an expert rope jumper in the generation before Tashi, thought I was a homeless lady—not, she quickly added, because of the way I dressed. In her neighborhood, a woman who is a constant fixture and not getting anyone in trouble is usually just homeless. Some children thought I was some kind of undercover narcotics officer. Others thought I was a news reporter. One thought I was Joey's mom, because I am white, like he is. One asked if I was from another country after hearing my New York accent. Another batted his eyelashes and asked if I was a new eighth-grader.

Like people everywhere, these children used images from their subculture to make sense of my strange role. I explained that I was a teacher and a writer and that I was trying to write down the games children play and the stories they tell because so many grown-ups seem to forget this important knowledge as they get older. The children nodded; this explanation made sense to them, although it still does not make much sense to me.

My handheld tape recorder and video camera served as story magnets; all of the tales presented in this chapter were spontaneously recorded and unsolicited. Although they demonstrate individual tellers' creativity, the story elements are of a particular time and place and are stylized in form and content. Too often considered exclusively psychological material, such tales are narratives of danger and bodily power, phantasmagoric and a lot like the children's neighborhoods and television sets.

Ironically, given its prevalence in childhood, children's spontaneous storytelling has rarely been recorded. The few published collections have focused on early childhood.[1] A particular psychological theoretical lens is typically superimposed on the stories, and the tales are used as a frame to illustrate Eriksonian or Piagetian theory. But the stories of the Mill School yard had little to do with industry or identity, although it is possible to make the case that aspects of the creations reflected both. The stories could be analyzed for their increasing complexity, but complex tales exist beside formulaic simple ones. Children's spontaneous storytelling demonstrates the teller's cleverness and subtle awareness of the strangeness of his or her environment.

There are many collections of older children's written narratives,[2] although a remarkable difference exists between what children of this age are able to write and what they are able to say. The engaging works of Robert Coles and Jonathon Kozol come closest to spontaneity, but fantasy and speech play are subtler than the nonfiction stories that ethnographers have traditionally collected.[3] Nonsense allows children to make their own kind of sense, a traditional form of communication that we grown-ups borrow from childhood.

These tales, in part sparked by the presence of the microphone, began suddenly, erupted in laughter, and then melted into the mix of game entry and exit. They were recorded on different days, told by different children in very different subcultures. The stories not only are culturally stylized but also have specific historical references; in this sense, they are not individual tales but tales of a cohort. The themes—bodily danger and warning, skill and victory—evolved into collaborative theater pieces where the players played off each other and their audiences. The stories were negotiated performances, teller and audience, text and context. The tellers are Tyron, Joey, Lilly, Kirsten, and Freddy—black, white, working class, middle class, male, and female.

In 1991, nine-year-old Tyron knew me as the "recess lady" and could not wait to tell a story into my portable microphone. He usually plays tag or handball, but this day, he just begins:

Tyron: This is Channel 6 News. Recess just starting. If you come new here, you're goin' to see the greatest stuff about to happen [laughter]. 'Cause, you know what's happening?
(What's happening?)
Tyron: [smiling] I'm about to kill somebody.
(Ooh.)
Tyron: Wanna know my name?
(Yeah.)
Tyron: It's called Fre-ddy. You gotta meet me—at the corner of *Pineapple* Street. And you gotta meeet me. And if you dare meet me, you'll never come back home. You'll be in [dramatic pause] Pet Sematary! Oohhhh!

Freddy, one of the names most associated with children's horror films, is not from the movie *Pet Sematary*, but this detail does not matter. Just like television, the movie advertisement comes right after the news, which itself shows what we currently find most fear-inducing. The surrealism of children's storytelling allows us to slip and slide from one frame into another; the news reporter introduces the killer, and the killer advertises the movie.

Joey, Karim, Marcus, and Billy, three African American boys and one European American boy, improvised their own news flash, sharing a pretend microphone. These hard-core handball players pause to tell me a tale:

Joey: Ten—no—5, 4, 3, 2, 1. This is Channel 6 News. Don't ever go to New York City. You will die just like [snaps fingers] that. You go to New York City, I'm a kick your butt, all right? So don't go-oh. [Karim comes into view] Oh, and something else. Don't let him talk. [Smile] He's crazy.
Karim: This is Channel 10 News—10, 9, 8, 7, 6, [faster] 5, 4, 3, 2, 1. Hello. It been an accident yesterday on the boulevard. Two cars and a truck hit each other. Car fell over and car blew up. That's it. No more newses today [giggles].
Marcus: This is Channel 3 News. 3, 2, 1. Don't you ever, ever, in your life go to California or you'll get shot. [Karim pushes him away; Billy enters]
Billy: You don't wanna be cool; don't stay in school.
Marcus: You wanna be cool; stay in school.
Karim: Don't do drugs. Drugs is for suckers [smiles].
Marcus: Don't use drugs. Drugs is for—

Karim: <u>Don't</u> use <u>drugs</u>. <u>Don't</u> believe the <u>hype</u> [bigger smile].
Marcus: <u>Don't</u> use <u>drugs</u>, 'cause they'll <u>kill</u> you [no smile].

This tale was recorded on June 1, 1992, while fires still burned in South-Central Los Angeles in response to racial injustice and the Rodney King verdict.[4] "Don't ever, ever in your life go to California or you'll get shot" is no random comment. "There was an accident on the boulevard . . ." "Don't do drugs, 'cause they'll kill you." The violent themes are simultaneously national, local, and in your face, moving seamlessly from news to public service announcement. The children are announcing their "newses," the multiple frameworks for their childhood.

In Philadelphia, across the country from Los Angeles, the children's stories, like their fears, are contextualized, framed by history and by cultural conventions of storytelling. Newspeak mixes with ethnically stylized urban African American speech and school public service announcements, paralleling the hybridity of their hand gestures—microphone holding, parental finger shaking, and teacherly pointing for emphasis. The media and grown-up culture bring the messages home, and the children play with it like sand from the beach.

Echoing the posters tacked on the concrete walls of the school building, the children slip into parody; the negative version is corrected by their peers. "You don't wanna be cool, don't stay in school." "You wanna be cool, stay in school." "Don't do drugs. Drugs is for suckers." "Don't do drugs 'cause they'll kill you." The message is that the cities will kill you, drugs will kill you, and your own family will hurt you if you get into trouble.

Lilly, tiny with long blond hair, offers her inverted prescription for fear in the form of a monster recipe. Lilly could often be seen as the lone white girl turning rope for her African American classmates doing double-dutch.

Lilly: There's a <u>big, giant</u> monster, in the <u>seven seas</u> [laughter]. [Another voice imitates a pirate] Arrgh Matey! It's Captain <u>Mush</u>! And I'm going to show you how to make <u>mush mud</u> pizza <u>pie</u>! One <u>vat</u> of water, two, two, two, two, <u>two</u> buckets of—
A boy: Two, two, two—

Lilly: Two buckets, two buckets of <u>dirt</u>! And, and for <u>topping</u>, chocolate-covered <u>ants</u>!
(Eww, mmm.)
Lilly: With wet <u>sand</u>!
(Mmm.)
Lilly: And then <u>mix</u> it. And it's <u>delicious</u>, I've <u>tried</u> it. [Pause] I'm the <u>monster</u>. I'm the <u>great</u>, <u>ugly</u>, <u>wet</u> ol' <u>mush mud</u> monster!

All three of these tales involve reversal, ambiguity, exaggeration, and danger—hallmarks of play.[5] Like a game, the telling of these tales is dramatic, competitive, and ritualized, shaped by the audience with an "argh," an "aye," a "two, two, two."

A handful of ten-year-old girls—black, white, and Asian—dawdle near the doorway. "Wanna hear a joke?"

A girl <u>telling</u> her <u>father</u> what she <u>learned</u> in <u>school</u>:
"A, B, C, D, E—ugh, ooh that <u>do</u> feel <u>good</u> to <u>me</u>."
"<u>What</u> did you <u>say</u>?"
"A, B, C, D, E—ugh, ooh that <u>do</u> feel <u>good</u> to <u>me</u>."
He <u>pushes</u> her into the <u>bath</u>room, <u>pulls</u> her pants <u>down</u>, <u>whips</u> her.
"A, B, C, D, E—ugh, ooh that <u>do</u> feel good to <u>me</u>."
"<u>What</u> did you <u>say</u>?"
"A, B, C, D, E—ugh, ooh that <u>do</u> feel <u>good</u> to <u>me</u>."
"<u>What</u> did you <u>say</u>?"
"A, B, C, D, E—ugh, ooh that <u>do</u> feel <u>good</u> to <u>me</u>."
He <u>whips</u> her <u>again</u>. "<u>What</u> did you <u>say</u>?"
"A, B, C, D, E—ugh, ooh you <u>beat</u> the <u>shit</u> out of <u>me</u>!"

The group giggles. One girl looks warily at me: "Ooh. A *curse* word!"
Already keenly aware of the strange relationship between punishment and sexuality, the girls eye me as they speak, giggling at their own use of taboo words. "Ooh. A *curse* word!" They were testing me as much as they were testing each other—it, too, was a story and a game. They made fun of both school and home and the confusingly different systems of punishment in the two places.

Reading these tales without hearing them or noting the laughter and the rhythmic emphasis would lead one to believe in a modern pathology of violence in children's imaginations. But psychologists of play Virginia Axline (1947), Erik Erikson (1950, 1975), Melanie Klein (1932/1975), and D. W. Winnicott (1971) do not see violence in the imagination itself as problematic;[6] rather, a lack of play signals depression, anxiety, and ill health in children. The stories are a form of cultural commentary about growing up scared and confused in a violent environment, and they utilize culturally stylized formats. Danger is out there on the seven seas, in California, in our homes, and on the corner of Pineapple Street. It is in our legends, in the news, in our fairy tales, in our formulaic poems, and in our games. It is the essence of a good drama.

Kirsten and her pale ten-year-old friends only mutter numbers when they jump rope. When I ask if they ever remember singing while they jump, Kirsten shakes her head and then offers:

> Tarzan, Tarzan in the _tree_
> Tree _split_ and he—
> What was the last one? [giggles]

She then improvises:

> The _queen_ is a _snake,_ the _king_ is a _jerk_
> The _jerk_ fell _down_ the stairs, _and_ the jerk _died_
> The _queen_ called the _cops, and_ the _cops came_
> The _cops_ fell _down_ the stairs
> The _queen_ got _arrested_
> 'Cause she _weren't_ in the _house_
> The _house_ burned _down_
> And the _queen_ had a _baby_
> The baby _died_ [laughter].

Kirsten's friend, Sheila, suggests, "Wasn't there that one about a fella?" "Cinderella!" hollers Kirsten, "Oh, I know that one."

> Cinderella [other girls join in]
> Dressed in yella

Went upstairs to see her fella
By mistake she kissed a snake
How many doctors did it take?

Then Sheila says, "Nah, we don't sing that one."

Better to sing nothing, say nothing, than to say things that are "corny," as the girls label songs that are out of date. The working-class white girls were witty enough and had memory enough, but in the early 1990s they had not found the words that could speak for them. They literally counted the time and the beats when they jumped rope—"101, 102." "Let's do numbers," they would say. "Let's do this one," they would gesture. The call to play was louder than the pat-pat-patting of the game itself. Over time, they found a way to speak using the borrowed words of the African American girls and the words of commercials, a meeting ground of common culture.

Games, like stories, tell about cultural tensions, cultural scripting, and the strangeness of growing up. As children pick and choose how to move their bodies and speak their words, they edit what is meaningful through exaggeration, minimalization, and negation in tone, volume, effort, shape, speed, and quality of touch.

Freddy, a smooth-talking, gifted African American athlete, explains the story behind his games:

In football season we play football. In basketball season, we play basketball.
In baseball season, we play baseball.

Given the spatial constraints of the school yard, basketball was played more than any other sport, and Roughhouse was the half-court folk game favorite. But the ten-year-old talk during these not-very-rough versions of Roughhouse was about sports stars and their shoes.

I got Reebok Walkers. You know Reebok Walkers?
Reebok Walkers.
I'm Michael Jordan.
I'm Shaquille O'Neal.
Let's play 21, y'all. Shoot Up, or Rough, or something.
(What do you usually play?)
Roughhouse or full.

(Sometimes you play full court?)

Yeah, let's play full court [gets excited].

You got Rod Strickland; he got Jordan, Kobe.

He got Rod Strickland. Kobe bangin', Kobe been bangin' [checks his pockets].

(Basketball cards?)

Uh huh. He done good [checks Kobe Bryant's statistics]. He's like— [moves dreamily, in slow motion, like he's faking the ball, like Kobe Bryant]. He fakes it like this and lays it up.

Basketball is not just basketball any more than the news is just the news or jump rope is just jump rope. Basketball here is a mix of hero play, fantasy, name-brand recognition, and skill. Exclusively for boys in 1991, the Mill School's sports games gradually accepted talented female players, and by 2002, girls were imitating WNBA stars, and groups of boys and girls were playing football during the run-up to the Super Bowl. All the stories and games undoubtedly had levels of which I, and perhaps the players, were unaware. What is significant is not the exposition of each layer but an acknowledgment that the layers exist and that they are, in this sample, explicitly culturally defined.[7]

The themes of the examples discussed to this point include death, food, sex, crime, pregnancy, and commercials, with their corresponding heroes. The gamestories condense time and location; leap associatively rather than linearly; blend logic with nonsense; decontextualize knowledge; have extreme emotion; are highly personal in symbolism; and are framed by cultural convention and events. In short, they sound much like dreaming. Playing, like dreaming, transforms reality into interesting and potentially meaningful bits of information. Both playing and dreaming have been described as having a subjunctive quality; they represent the hypothetical world "as if." Jean Piaget, the great scholar of children's cognition, has written, "It would be difficult in our opinion not to recognize these dreams and the games of the same children, the one difference being that: in dream symbolism there are nightmares, while in ludic symbolism fear is still enjoyed."[8]

As the dream literature has moved beyond Sigmund Freud's notion of dreams as "wish fulfillment," the play literature is just now moving past the Eriksonian parallel of play as mere "mastery." Both frameworks offered exciting new ways of thinking about play. For Erikson, who focused on the therapeutic play of young children, play gives a sense of "divine leeway, of excess space." Play is "an attempt to synchronize the bodily and social processes with the self."[9] In a sense, play is social dreaming.

Freud has written, "Might we not say that every child at play behaves like a creative writer, in that he creates a world of his own, or rather, rearranges the things of his world in a new way which please him? . . . May we really attempt to compare the imaginative writer with the dreamer in broad daylight."[10]

The vast field of dream research, which is divided over the centrality of meaning in dreams and even whether dreams reflect anything meaningful, parallels a central debate about play. Does the nonsense of play make sense, or is it random symbolism? Does playground activity have meaning, and if it does, what consequences does that meaning have in terms of recess policy? Does play parallel creativity, or is play the source of creativity, as Freud suggested? If play, like dreams, is random and meaningless although entertaining, as J. Allan Hobson and David Foulkes suggest, what do the texts of play tell us about culture?[11]

Whether the play represents meaning to the children or not, it does allow observers to peek inside children's heads. What anthropologists David Shulman and Guy Stroumsa have written about dreams could easily describe play and games: "By their very liminality . . . they permit, where other media fail, a way of intra-cultural communication of great flexibility."[12] Play, like a dream, is an in-between state, and play, like sleep, is at its deepest when it is dreamlike. One only needs to try to prevent a child from playing to experience something of the intensity of this mental state. Children often need "waking up" from their play or game, gentle guidance back to reality. But after a fine bout of play, Erikson has written, children "appear satiated and relaxed as in waking from a satisfying dream."[13] Brian Sutton-Smith goes further: "Play is, as it were, a halfway house between the night and the day, the brain and the world."[14]

G. William Domhoff questions dreams' functioning but acknowledges that "the evidence suggests that they have at least some coherence and meaning" and that "the continuity between dream content and waking life is one of the most striking findings." He continues, "People dream most about the people and interests that preoccupy them in waking life."[15]

Beyond the hypothetical question of whether dreaming resembles play, and beside their similar cultural and emotional framings, the biggest difference between the two is control. In play, the surreal emotional/cultural fragment can be started or stopped by the player or by someone else. And play, as flexible as a dream, is multimodal, with words, tones, bodies, space, and time up for variation. Above all, play is social. These spontaneous tales were interrupted, added to, shaped by more than just the teller. "You don't wanna be cool, don't stay in school"; "Two, two, two"; "Yeah, let's play full court." Laughter, excitement, encouragement, and discouragement shape the performances at play, as do a host of contextual influences.

To speak of the cultural frame of play in all its potential surrealism means making a sort of virtual Venn diagram of the children's worlds. At the center are the games and stories, floating in and out of each other, overlapping like liquid. They are at the center because the children put them at the center of their daily lives. Tyron, Lilly, Karim, and their friends guided me to see their school yard in game-story units: the places where jump rope would take place, the basketball court, the invisible third hoop between the two half courts, the hopscotches, the spots used for wrestling, and the lone tree that served as both home base and a place for pretending. The stories erupted in between these markers as the children bounced their way into new games or stunts.

Surrounding these partially visible zones of games and stories was the institution of school, with its metal fences and whistle-blowing aides. Beyond were the overlapping frameworks of gender roles and ethnicity, race, and social class, influencing what was permissible and how the games and stories were to be played. These frameworks, in turn, were framed by the local geographies of the school neighborhood—pawnshops, trucks and places where tradespeople worked or bought donuts, and a dry cleaner whose sign read, "Unemployed? We will clean your interview suit for free." Pulling back still further reveals the neighborhoods from which the poorer children were bused in, where pharmacies advertised not union plans but food stamps, where drug dealing was out in the open. An even broader perspective encompasses national culture—movies, pop music, commerce, and the news.

If we accept that the children's stories are cultural tales and that it is a short leap from storytelling to gametelling, then the stage is set to examine the games of the school yard as dreamy cultural pieces. The task is to collect the game stories as earnest, albeit sometimes silly, cultural fragments. Folklorist Iona Opie writes, "One of the aims of collecting school lore is to assemble enough data to see into the minds of the children of a particular era, their preferences and the reasons for those preferences."[16] Psychologist Jerome Bruner concurs: "The power to create reality, to reinvent culture, we will come to recognize, is where a theory of development must begin its discussion of mind."[17] But to find meaning in these cultural collections, these negotiated inventions, we must first examine the assumptions of the collecting process.

Books of children's games typically list the games in digest form, and the reader cannot tell which games were preferred and which were only rarely performed.[18] So many collections of tales, songs, and games ignore the popular nature of folk culture; what is loved may be kept private or sung daily, because people have different ways of cherishing their favorite artifacts. Most quantitative studies are so focused on numbers that children's lives are reduced to formulas and graphs—charts where living people once played. The result is myopic views of individual children and telescopic views of the abstractions of childhood, with very little in between. The task ahead is to quantify what is essentially a qualitative study.[19]

If we take one record from Grandmother's attic, but it was only listened to once and was not liked by anyone and present it on the same plane as a loved collection that was played daily, we are presenting a warped picture of that time and place. But Grandmother's wedding dress is worn only once. Merit does not rest solely on frequency alone. Markers in time or place or passion have differing value systems. A festival happens once a year, and festive songs and clothes are significant dramatic markers of a particular culture. But people rarely wear their festival clothes and sing their festival songs on a daily basis. To describe people as doing so distorts the picture. Both Sui and Fly Girl are favorite games, but only one is also popular. Tag is a favorite but not played nearly as much as basketball. There is passion, and there is frequency.

Audio and video enable us to record multiple things at the same time and repeatedly to examine what is before us (thereby increasing our reliability); these technologies also can verify the consistency of our logical categories (validity). We can have a large sample (wide angle) and a detailed, dramatic view (zoom lens). We can keep variables relatively the same (one school yard during recess) and see how things change over time and space. We can gather everything seen and heard and give honor to the most cherished.[20] What emerges is more than a collection of ditties and stories, more than a chart. It is a way of thinking about children's games, their potential meaning, and the culture of power. It leads us to the significance of the body as a site for cultural negotiation and to the significance of the words of games, at their loudest and most frequent, as flags of cultural tension.

Part 2

THE
PUSH AND PULL
OF
ADULT CULTURE

- 3 -

THE GROWN-UPS GIVETH, THE GROWN-UPS TAKETH AWAY
Misunderstanding Gendered Play

In 1992, Mikee Cohen, a popular, pale-faced ten-year-old with dark eyes, was an expert in handball. He heard that I was interviewing children during recess time to ask about their school yard games. He followed me one morning and began to interview me:

> **Mikee**: Where are you from?
> (Do you mean what planet?)
> **Mikee**: I know you are from Earth, but really, are you from Israel or someplace?
> (No, I grew up in New York, but I live in Philadelphia in Northtown.)
> **Mikee**: I'm from Easttown.
> (Oh, I know Easttown, I've visited people there.)
> **Mikee**: Do you know Mikee Cohen?
> (Is that you?)
> **Mikee**: No, my dad.
> (No, I'm afraid I don't. I don't know a lot people from Easttown.)
> **Mikee**: Did you know Deborah Cohen? She's my mom. She died.
> (Shakes head; long silence.)

Mikee: Will you pick me tomorrow? [looks smaller, more childlike than usual]
(I'll pick the first to volunteer.)
Mikee: Will you pick me?
(I pick whoever volunteers.)
Mikee: Then you'll pick me.
(Yes [pause]. You better run and get back to class. I don't want to get you in trouble.)
Mikee: [Leaves, smiling].

I interviewed anyone who wanted to be interviewed in small groups by game type. We would go into a small, unused classroom during recess, usually only on rainy days, unless the teacher had other plans. Some children, like Mikee, had a lot to say about their games. The games—handball, hopscotch, wrestling—were very important to the children, much more than their teachers knew. Mikee knew how to negotiate with me and to negotiate with his peers. I did my best to negotiate with them through humor; at times their responses were sobering.

No matter their gender, race, social class, or ethnicity, the children described the school yard as a time for showing what you're the best at and demonstrating what you know. Playing these games involves both physical balance and the intentional challenging of one's perceptions and the balancing of one's needs and skills along with everyone else's. The children negotiated time (turn taking), space (game occupation), possession of objects, defense of status, and defense of friendship. They also negotiated with all the adults in their play space (the aides) and the adults about to end the playtime (the teachers). Moreover, individuals negotiated groups by game genre (hopscotch, rope, ball, Sui), and identity (race, ethnicity, gender, class, and age). Disorientation, though misunderstood by the adults, is essential to the dynamics of such game play. The command "Challenge, challenge" in the jump rope games was echoed by "Challenge, challenge" in the handball game and was muttered by the adults in the school yard, who shook their heads, "Challenge, challenge."

This chapter examines three beloved games of the Mill School yard (handball, hopscotch, and the Fighting Game) as well as a host of improvised toys and spontaneous play with leaves and snow. All of these activities involved peer negotiation and demonstrate the adults' larger misunderstandings of the significance of play. The games fell under the direct control of grown-ups, who had the power to disallow, ignore, or sanction games in ways that rendered them unplayable.

Like jump rope, steps, or hopscotch, the ball games were fiercely loved, and the children often imagined themselves as the games' inventors. The fourth-grade boys announced:

We made it up.
We made it up.
Just like we made up [this] and all those other games.

Yet the fifth-grade boys also claimed to have invented the games:

But we be, like, our class—all of us—made up all the games.

Jean Piaget has claimed that the moral universe of childhood is invented and played out in children's struggle with their games.[1] Based on his study of the Swiss game of marbles, the marbles and their circular hand-drawn frame give children the opportunity to create rules, debate them, and argue their position in their microworld. At the center of Piaget's conversations with children is the idea of invented justice, fair and foul, at play. Like pragmatist educator John Dewey, Piaget believed that the child's world had to be invented, re-created, to achieve understanding. The boys of the Mill School concur: "We made it up. We made up all them games." The children owned the games.

Piaget studied games as legitimate social institutions and collected stories about how the games were played—a metaanalysis of play, done with the children themselves. His rival, L. S. Vygotsky, wrote of mind in society, of play as a "zone" where children push themselves and are pushed to higher levels of skill and complexity within a particular cultural context.[2] I was curious about how the children made sense of the microworlds of play as play itself changes over time. How are play traditions like tools? Beyond changing the texts of singing games, how do children traditionally negotiate power in their changing world? How do children negotiate meaning, frequency, and sequencing?[3] We turn our attention to the beloved folk games of handball, hopscotch, wrestling, and tag, games of the body where words are secondary.

HANDBALL

Mikee is an expert at wall ball, loved by the nine-year-old boys. It involves throwing a tennis ball high against the school building, with no bouncing. The one who neatly catches the ball gets to be the next thrower. Mikee's buddy, Malik, tall and lean, said his favorite was step ball, which used to be known as stoop ball, in which the ball is bounced off the lunchroom steps. Darnell's favorite was Chink, or Chinese handball, an alley handball game for two, like wall tennis. The players had no knowledge that *Chink* was a racial epithet. One student guessed that the game had been made up by Chinese people, while another suggested that the name came from hitting a piece, or chink, in the wall. Ironically, school yard handball has always been integrated in terms of race, ethnicity, and social class.[4]

Without a doubt, the most popular handball game at the Mill School was Sui. Like Piaget's marbles, Sui has a boundary, has moving targets, and is based on the principle of attack and defense. It took me three-quarters of the year to find out that the name *Sui* is short for *Suicide*, a handball game so revered and so symbolically dangerous that it has been officially outlawed in the school yard. Not that it stopped anyone.

Sui was violent in a theatrical way and involved the sanctioned pegging, "beaming," or "beaning" of the other players. To be safe, a player who inadvertently touches the ball must run up and touch the wall and shout, "Sui!" When I asked why some people said they were good at some handball games but not others, Mikee replied that it is "what they know." "'Cause people don't have to aim in Sui," said Darnell, taking pride in his Chink game. "'Cause if they get hit with the ball, they cry," said Malik, and all of the boys laughed. Skill is a combination of what one knows and what risks one can handle, an interplay of cultural knowledge and emotional strength.[5] Special terms for Sui include "relay" and "no relay," which allows the ball to be thrown from a far person to a near person, who then tags another player with the ball. "Challenge" means that the ball must be thrown from a particularly difficult place. Most of all, the word *Sui* was a magical protector—touching the base wall provided protection from being beamed if a player accidentally touched or was touched by the ball. At times, the ball would be lobbed and neatly caught, with no shouts and no pegging. But the excitement of the game came from the unpredictability of potential danger. Safety meant being alert.

> Yeah, they bean the stew out of you.
> *You then sayin', "I ain't playin', I ain't playin.'" That's what I do.*
> **Don't raise no shorts.**
> (So if you don't want to do it, and you're going to get beaned anyway, you just say, "I ain't playin,'" and then it doesn't count, right?)
> *Yeah, but they still beam you [giggles].*
> (Do you beam the people you like, or the people you don't like?)
> Everybody!
> *Everybody!*
> **Everybody!**

The children had their own boundaries for what was fair, even in a mock violent game. They also explained Homicide, a game described but never played at school.

> *You had to walk the wall like this and then ball hits you and you got to get out of the way. They gonna beam you, you be like—smack, pow, smack. That's no fun, That ain't no fun.*
> Yeah, like they hit people and all, Homicide.

Although even Sui can sound dreadful, it is actually a slight variation of an "old school" classic, still taught in gym classes, known as dodgeball or gaga. In dodgeball, however, the ball is large and red and bouncy; Suicide uses tennis balls. Students told tales of a time when golf balls were used. Yet Suicide, as drastic as the game sounds, is pretty mild when played with a tennis ball.

Sui was not allowed in gym. "In gym!" they laughed. "You'd get suspended for playing Sui in gym." The game was typically played in the three-walled alley between the buildings, limiting the space for runaway balls and providing shelter from critical grown-up eyes. Sui was allowed in 1992 but was banned in 1999, when the children who weren't playing taunted:

Oh, you just <u>did</u> it. You're gonna get in <u>trouble</u>.
You're not allowed to play [Sui]. Anyway, you'ze do.
(Are you not allowed to play wall ball?)
You're allowed to play wall ball, but you're not allowed to play Homicide.
Sui.
Whatever.
It's got always to be pegging. It's got always to be pegging. That's the fun, the fun. <u>Boom!</u> [mocks a crashing fall]

I laugh with the boys playing ball on another side of the building and admire their heroic catches. "You're playing wall ball? Do they let you play Sui, or are you not allowed?" "Naw, wall ball." A boy makes a splendid one-handed catch. Another shouts, "He grabbed it out of the sky. It's a bird. It's a plane. It's Richieeee!" Another boy gracefully jumps over a short fence, almost flying with both legs parallel to the ground before he lands effortlessly to retrieve a ball. An aide yells at him for doing something "dangerous." At the same time, a potential fight begins to intensify, but no adult notices.

Sui's origin may have nothing to do with suicide. An unfortunate name, it does add to the drama. Children have been taught to do "suicide drills" in gym, running many times back and forth between two lines. Sui's origins likely lie in Sooey ("sau ball" or pig ball), a European stick-and-can game of elimination.[6] The swineherd tries to knock the pig (the can or ball) into a hole after the rest of the players run to a specific place, yell "Sooey," and run back. Calling Sui *Suicide* is a bit of folk etymology, celebrating the mild level of danger associated with the game. Elsewhere in Philadelphia, Sui is known as Polish handball.

(Does it hurt when you get beamed?)
Yeah, <u>sometimes</u>.
<u>Naah</u>. <u>Not</u> sometimes, when you got on two pair of jeans [laughter] like I do. It don't hurt me.
Especially when they beam 'em.
(Do you have to hit from below the waist? Is that the deal? Or it doesn't matter?)
Anywhere.
Anywhere.

Anywhere.
In the arm, but not in the head.
(Not in the head.)
I know, but they duck, they duck, they duck.
Don't—do not wear shorts if you want to play some Sui.
I gave him a haircut on the last one [laughter].
I jump. Nobody could hit me.

The boys loved telling tales of their handball skills and even of their sillier inventions, like Dick against the Wall. "'Cause the person had to go up to the wall, and *only* boys could play, and then they go up to the wall [giggles] and put their dick on the wall [laughter]." "Yeah! [more laughter]" They would joke about making each other look silly and tell tales about sneaking up on the roof to retrieve lost balls.

(What is your favorite game of all of them? Do you have one favorite?)
Sui!
Sui!
Sui!

That gendered bodily play would emerge in Sui was an interesting phenomenon. In 1999, mixed-gender games of Suicide Handball and wall ball took place—a hybrid of tag, flirting, rough play, and the game itself. In addition, two cliques of girls regularly played all-girl Sui games.

Susie: We play Sui and wall ball.
Mary: This is only my second time playing! [Bob smacks Susie with an empty plastic soda bottle.]
Julie: Freebie [tosses the ball high in the air, and all the players try to get it; Bob tries to kick Mary; she chases him].
Joe: Ahhh [sighs]. He likes her.

Only once during the 1991–92 school year did a girl dare to play Sui, and she did not repeat the attempt. In 1999, female Sui players were common, although a stigma (sometimes proudly worn) still went with being a girl Sui player: "We play . . . 'cause we're tomboys. At least me and Jen are." One of the boys confessed softly that he plays Sui with his sister at home. Playing "boy" games with girls was clearly a touchy subject.

In 1999, I asked the girls who tend to play Sui what they liked to play during recess.

We like to play hopscotch, basketball, hide and seek, Sui, wall ball.
(The guys let you play basketball?)
[quickly] No [laughter].
They play football, basketball, chase the girls.
The girls play chase the boys, and the boys—
(What do the girls do?)
We started playin' Sui, but Mr. Mann [the armed security guard] took the ball away from us, sayin' we can't do that 'cause people get bopped.

In Piaget's time, girls did not play boys' games, and his developmental framework of stages of morality found no complicated parallel in the games of girls. Yet today, Sui is an up-and-coming girls' game, validating the crossover that women now have in the workforce, and the boys goofily play at keeping girls out. The girls then bring their own balls from home, on guard for the boys' intrusions and the skeptical eye of Mr. Mann.

As Mr. Mann walks by the girls' Sui game, he and the players stop and stare at each other. For one minute, they all freeze. The girls then toss their heads, try to act casual, and continue to play their own, slightly calmer version of the outlawed game.

For all the players, Sui is about two things: keeping score and survival. Overall, Sui is about power, and it is no coincidence that more and more young girls are braving these more dangerous games and more boys are accepting female players. Ironically, Sui is a double game of power—with both the ball and with the grown-ups in charge.

The grown-up distaste for Sui seemed to be related to the idea of pegging, yet chase and escape—attack and defense—is the core of almost every competitive game. Baseball had been outlawed in the early 1990s and was the initial reason for the cancellation of recess at the Mill School after a child was accidentally beaned with the ball. Like the Fighting Game, which was a boxing-ring game of pushing, Sui was self-selecting, and the drama was more evident in the storytelling than in the actual game. I never had to take a child who had been playing Sui to the nurse, but I earned my keep by carrying children to the nurse after they got hurt lining up when the bell rang.

In 2004, the alleyway is blocked off by a forbidding, bright orange cone. No play of any kind is allowed there anymore. The new security guard, kinder than the other, talks about the games as little children run and dance around him. He is a mobile base, a safety point, and he good-naturedly talks while dodging little ones. He does not like or allow "wall tag," "that game of pegging." Regular tag is now called "hit and run," but he does not seem to mind that name. The children nonchalantly play wall ball on the side of the building, as they have always done. But when they think no adults are looking, the game turns back into the still-revered Sui.

The new officer notices a big group forming two lines facing each other. One girl suggests that they might be doing a Fighting Game. He scowls and goes over to investigate. They are in fact elaborately picking teams for football—the Eagles are in the National Football League play-offs. He shakes his head and says, "You do all this to pick a team? You only got five minutes. Hurry up or you won't have any time to play!" For children, the pregame ceremony is as important as the game itself.[7] It is the ritual of negotiation of power within a context that itself is negotiating its power.

HOPSCOTCH

For a subset of the Mill School's female population, every recess was an opportunity to play hopscotch. As chalk drawings were outlawed, the girls only began playing in April 1991, when Mr. Bee, the gym teacher and school disciplinarian, officially painted the two hopscotches. A huge crowd of little girls sagely offered him advice, rolling their eyes as he attempted to fill in the spaces with the wrong numbers. Pigtailed third-graders Jenny and Susie bounced as they remembered exactly when the diagrams were painted:

(It was painted by Mr. Bee just a month or two ago—)
Jenny: Not even.
(Not even. What did you guys do before that?)
Susie: We would just—I would just walk around. Boring.

And a group of fifth-grade girls shouted:

Janet: Every recess we play hopscotch.
(Every recess. I know that most of the stuff I'm going to show you [on video] today is you guys playing hopscotch. Most of you [group giggles]. I noticed they didn't have a hopscotch painted until just a month or two ago.)
Janet: Yeah.
Debbie: Yeah.
Vicky: Mr. Bee.
Debbie: Mr. Bee painted it.
(Mr. Bee painted it. And you all stood around and were telling him how to do it, because he didn't know how to do it, right [group giggles]? So what did you do before there was a hopscotch?)
Vicky: Sit on the wall. Play with the boys.
Trish: Beat them up.
(Beat up the boys, and you sat on the wall.)
Debbie: Running, running.

The game offered the girls a diversion not only from boredom but from acts of aggression. Without the negotiation that the game provides, the girls lapsed into boredom and passivity. The addition of hopscotch was a major change in the play activity of these young girls. Each day, most of the European American girls and many of the middle-class African American girls would try to get into a hopscotch game. In addition to ethnic integration, the game provided a new social space in which girls talked, shared snacks, and hung out, even if they were not playing. The paint literally changed the shape of the social space and, at least initially, centralized it like no other. These girls hopped to get there, hopped to get back into school, and could be seen sneaking hops in the hallway.

Piaget, brilliant in his groundbreaking study of the boys' games marbles and his theory of moral judgment, dismissed hopscotch in French-speaking Switzerland as simplistic. He believed that the game "never presents the splendid codification and the complicated jurisprudence of the game of marbles." "It is sufficient to show that in the main the legal sense is far less developed in little girls."[8] This unfortunate assessment contributed to the misunderstanding of girls' cognition among a whole generation of scholars in the field of moral development, yet Piaget's main discovery in this study remains underappreciated—that within the realm of children's games lies a whole society. The game is a vital process of digesting knowledge about the larger social world.

Hopscotch has existed for a very long time. Folklorists Iona and Peter Opie have documented it in mid-eighteenth-century England; Simon Bronner, citing J. W. Crombie, dates it to the mid–seventeenth century; and Mary and Herbert Knapp write that "a hopscotch diagram can still be seen on the pavement of the Roman Forum."[9] In most places around the world, the game's shape constantly varies. The game is the Bell in Italy, the Temple in Austria, and in Italy, the last three divisions are Inferno, Purgatorio, and Paradiso.[10] Whether the game is known as potsie or hoppy, any scholarly emphasis has consistently focused on the drawing of the board, the hopping movement, and the game distribution rather than on game entry, style, or legal battles. Since the figure was permanently drawn in the Mill School yard by an adult male, we must look at movement and speech for localized variations in meaning. The game lay not in the drawing but in the rule making.

As sociologist Erving Goffman has noted,[11] the interaction is the game, yet the frame of the game must be studied to understand the interaction. Nevertheless, most studies of games have focused on them as fixed lists of rules or have generalized about gender or race based on one particular case study. Adding Goffman's notions of frame analysis and the performance of interaction to the ethnographic tool box was a significant leap for me, providing a chance to see games as living examples of specific subcultures in specific historical contexts.

At the Mill School, two hopscotches served a population of several hundred girls. No boys played the game, although a few crashed through it during chase games. Two simultaneous hopscotch games took place, each usually with four to six players. Each player had her own "man" or "marker," "piece," "stick," or "guy," generally a found object—a stick, cigarette butt, or bottle cap—or a personal item, such as keys or a pen. Each player in turn would stand at the base and toss her marker into the number 1 box. Then she would have to hop or jump onto each number, without stepping on a line or a box with a marker in it, usually hopping on 1, then jumping on 2, turning around on 10, and returning the same way. If successful, she would then toss her marker on 2 and repeat the pattern until she missed. Then another player would take her turn.

Above all, hopscotch is a game of balance and the testing of territorial boundaries.

> You can't step on a line.
> *You can do it by accident, but if you do it on purpose, you're out.*
> **You try to throw it.**
> You can't step if someone's stick is there.
> You have to throw it to the next one.

The game became more complicated as each person progressed because the rules stipulated that any box with a marker in it could not be stepped on or touched. As more players threw their markers, the players would have to hop rather than jump, sometimes far, to retrieve their guys. In addition, real trash and unintentional markers often rested on the hopscotch, confusing the quickly hopping player. Out of the confusion comes "helpsies"—literally an act of lifting up a player and placing her where she needs to be.

Helpsies is one of a whole slew of "new rules" used by the Mill School's third-, fourth-, and fifth-grade girls. The female teachers were baffled by helpsies, which they had never seen before. An ethnically diverse group of third-graders discussed the game:

> (Folks, let me ask you some things about hopscotch. I've seen people play with various different rules that I never saw before.)
> Kinda like walksies and helpsies.
> (Like walksies and helpsies—right. First of all, what's walksies again?
> *Walksies is when like—*
> Wait, wait, make pretend these blocks are the hopscotch. You just walk [demonstrates].
> (Uh huh. Does anybody ever play with walksies?)
> *Yeah.*
> Yeah.
> (Sometimes you do.)
> And helpsies is like, sometimes, like, people don't know, like, if there's pieces on something or on, like, 6 and you have to get all the way to 1, and people, like, do lift them and put them on 1.
> (Do you play with walksies and helpsies?)

Not all the time.

(No?)

Other people do.

And do you know what red, white, bluesies are?

(Tell me about red, white, bluesies.)

It's like when you start and you get going on, like, 4 or 5, you walk, you go like red-white-blue. Then you put down the piece.

Sometimes they say, when you get til 4, then you can do it, but sometimes they say on 5.

And if you're doing 4, you have to get on the line, and you want to get on 4, you have to go—

[Students together] Red, white, blue.

And then sometimes have bendsies, and you can just go like that and put your piece on 1 and then you can start.

(Okay. Now, do you have to call bendsies before the game starts?)

Yeah, you have to call everything.

(You have to call everything before the game starts.)

You have to call everything that you want in the game.

(Got it. Got it.)

Before the game start, 'cause if you called it in the middle, then, then it doesn't count; all already started to already do it.

Although the game was fixed in dried paint, the girls made the game flexible through the rules. Power was reconfigured in the hands of those who started the game, who could call the rules they wanted. Contrary to Piaget's observation, this game was all about rules and their negotiation, even when no talking was taking place.

Yeah, a lot of times we just don't talk a lot. When we're playing, just trying to remember what number we just come off of.

(When you're playing, you have to concentrate.)

Someone should be watching her, she could cheat. I'm looking at her, see if she's cheating.

After observing the occasional argument and the potential for meanness in their accusations, I asked the fifth-grade girls about refusing helpsies as they watched themselves on tape.

(Now, can people refuse to help you? Like, someone says, "No, I'm not going to help you?")

Yeah.

Yeah.

Yes.

If you call no helpsies.

You have to call helpsies if you need help.

(Oh.)

And you have to call red, white, blue, and you have to call big steps, and—

But you have to call them at the beginning of the game so everybody knows, and it's not just when friends you have need it.

And two hands if you need two hands to pick up.

But we usually call one hand.

(One hand?)

Yeah, like this. But it's hard to go, like that.

(Now, do you have to stay on the same foot the whole time?)

[shakes head, murmurs a disagreement] Just when there's switching, if they call switching.

If they say no switching feet, you can't switch.

(Oh, so that's probably why it's hard, too, for someone to enter in the middle of the game—because they don't know what was called. Right?)

Yeah.

(They won't know if someone said no walksies.)

And then—

And then they wouldn't know what you were playing.

And then a lot of people are ahead of them, they'd be on 1, and we're like on 8 or something.

(Uh-huh. That's true. They'd never catch up.)

And if you had too many people in there, it's hard 'cause you gotta jump far.

I know, and they, they get more people, and we don't know who else is playing.

Although both groups emphasized the importance of the rules and the fairness involved in calling all the special rules at the beginning, the fifth-graders used almost twice as many rules or terms as the third-graders.

I next turn to two video clips that deal with power, passivity, territoriality, and the relevance of language and body movement to ownership. They were filmed during the first week in June 1991, in the year the hopscotches were painted. The girls are keenly aware both of the other players and of a nearby group of girls who are interested in playing.

	Left Hopscotch	Voices	Right Hopscotch	Outsiders
10:30:04	Girl tosses her marker and steps in the space.	"You're out!"		
	She touches space again anyway.			
10:30:12			Girl has returned to number 1.	Third-grade girls run and stand by
10:30:15	Stillness		Stillness	Stillness
10:30:20	Next girl tosses.			
10:30:23			Girl tosses and jumps.	
10:30:26				Third-graders retreat
10:30:38	Girl goes.		Girl returns.	Third-graders retreat more, begin to eat
10:30:45			Red, white, bluesies	
10:30:48			Girl tosses and jumps	
10:30:52	Girl tosses and jumps.			Third-graders retreat more
10:30:56	Girl pauses		Girl pauses	

There is a ripple effect of passivity here. The hopscotches are permanently drawn, so only two groups can play. The two groups can only include a limited number of players, so the younger girls end up eating. An even broader territoriality is evident in the next exchange, which focuses on only one game.

	Hopscotch	Voices
10:47:06	Girl begins her turn, and a second girl jumps simultaneously on the same board, a few numbers behind her, because the bell is about to ring.	
10:47:28		You stepped on 7!
	First hopper pauses. [Critic calmly demonstrates]	You went like this—
10:47:34	They all pause, a boy jumps onto the hopscotch and does a fast version of pretend hopscotch.	
10:47:38	Previous hopper pushes him off.	[Bell sounds]
10:47:39	Arms are raised	First next game!
10:47:40		Second!
10:47:41		Third!

When I showed the third-graders the hopscotch tapes, I asked if they also negotiate who goes first or second before they get outside. They replied with a resounding yes. After watching themselves running to play hopscotch on videotape, the fifth-graders talked to me about what they saw:

> (So you guys really ran out there fast to get the board.)
> **Yeah.**
> *Yeah.*
> Yeah, but they always beat us.
> (Do they?)
> *At lunch time they beat us 'cause their teacher lets them out that door.*
> (Ahhh.)
> *The [closer] recess door.*

At the end of the same interview, the subject of taking turns again came up:

> Is it time to get ready?
> **I'm first.**
> First.
> (Huh?)
> Sec—

Second.
What time is it?
Third.
Aw, I'm gonna be last?
(It's ten of.)
How mean.
It's recess now, isn't it?
(You're calling numbers now to play hopscotch?)
Yeah.
Is recess over?
If we can get out there . . .

The children can negotiate ahead of time among themselves only up to a point, for limits are imposed by the permanent hopscotch, the teacher who sets up strategically near the door, the girls who get there first and choose who plays, and the rule that additional players cannot join after the game has begun. The players have the options of fighting, arguing, or withdrawing. In this case, withdrawing can mean becoming even more passive and likely eating and not moving.

The girls said that fights take place over the hopscotch territory. How to solve this problem? "There should be one for each class," offered one third-grader. The fifth-graders suggested three, four, or five hopscotches. Ironically, painting the hopscotches opened up a new opportunity for play at recess, activating a whole population of girls, but also made obvious the passive role left for the girls who are of lower status or who are less lucky in their arrival time in the school yard.[12]

In 1999, four more hopscotches were painted near the opposite side of the school yard, in an open area not far from the building. Some sporadic play took place there, but the children found the placement too vulnerable. In 2004, I did not see any children using them, and chalk was still not allowed. Well-intentioned help in the playground is sometimes misplaced. The children need to participate in the creation of their game worlds.

Only one fifth-grade girl mentioned playing hopscotch after school at her local recreation center. There, the game was called Poison and was the same officially painted board, only smaller, with even more flexible rules, easier throwing, and easier hopping. This suggests a possible correlation between the fixing of the paint and the limitations in rule flexibility. This idea is relevant to the larger argument that rigidity in one area tends to lead to flexibility in another if it is allowed.

School officials unknowingly controlled the games in a structural way by limiting access to materials and then painting on the concrete. Yet the girls compensated by creating flexible rules for flexible bodies. Some structures set children up more fairly than others, but assuming structural determinism would be as simpleminded as assuming that children, especially girls, have access to real "free play" at school.

What is striking is the creativity associated with restrictions, the passion articulated, and the ability of a seemingly simple game to reflect patterns of power in school culture. The fifth-graders rarely play the game at home, but "every recess we play hopscotch." They arch and bend with grace and move along their path. They even lift each other up when times are hard—negotiating space, negotiating turns, negotiating gendered play.

THE FIGHTING GAME

Next to the original hopscotches, Mr. Bee also painted a square for a ball-bouncing game that no one ever plays. Instead, the children line up for the Fighting Game and use the boundaries as the ring for professional wrestling. The idea is to push someone out of the boundary, even by a little, and then the other is the winner.

The fighting arena was in constant use from 1991 to 2004. Smaller, weaker students often would challenge larger ones, and the setting provided a place where outcast students could regain status and honor in the school yard. Older boys would gently tap a chosen player to begin the round. The winner would play a new challenger, with challengers selecting themselves. Students were thrown to the ground; the gym teacher said that although mats would have provided some protection, the school's budget would not permit officials to risk damage to or the disappearance of the mats.

The children wrestle while standing on the cement. Taking advantage of the camera presence, Edgar, one of my constant companions, narrates and instructs, switching fluidly from role to role.

We have the next match coming up. And the next match will be these two, blue and white versus purple and white. And it looks like blue and white is winning. [Pauses, changes tone while watching the two hopping on one foot, one in the square, one out.] You can't have both feet up at once. Once your body's out, you're out. It's tremendous. We have another winner.

That winner is pigtailed Jenny.

The children create moments of negotiation through the traditional frames of handball, hopscotch, and the wrestling ring, through counting out, singing, and arguing. Adults interfere, using their power to set the stage for opportunity and lack of opportunity. Sui is prohibited, yet it thrives. Hopscotch is at first not permitted but is eventually sanctioned, though constrained. Yet the children have over time found their way, crying fair or foul, in or out, safe or not safe, it or not it. As they holler, their bodies negotiate. Your turn, my turn. Relay, no relay. Safe. Out. Challenge, challenge.

Categories of girls' games and boys' games prove fluid, as girls adopted Sui and the Fighting Game. The school yard is a host for subtle cultural change, often unsanctioned, scorned by the grown-ups in charge. Game spaces live and die, change players, and change names, but the genres, the game forms, appear to have more staying power.

BEYOND GENDER: NEGOTIATING TOYS

The children of the Mill School were allowed few props in the yard, so nature's toys were much in demand. On fall days when the lone tree shed its bounty, the yard turned into a festival of leaf games. Hide in the Pile, Leaf Wars, Jump in the Pile, Stuff Your Friend's Shirt with Leaves, Fake Snow, and simple Leaf Crunching frenetically took over, replacing most rope and ball games. But as soon as all the leaves fell, the grumbling custodian placed them in plastic bags to be hauled away, much to the disappointment of the children. Safety was cited as the reason for the removal of the leaves.

In winter, the children were outside in all types of weather, as mandated by the school district, and eagerly awaited any sign of snow. A snowy yard meant sneaky snowball fights, snow sculptures, stuff your friend's shirt with snow, snowfall simulations, and if you were lucky, pretend ice skating. The next day the grumbling lone custodian had shoveled. Again, school officials cited safety as the reason.

Spring brought gypsy moth caterpillars to the lone tree, and 1999 was a particularly bountiful year. Almost all of the fourth- and fifth-graders, from the biggest tough guys to the smallest and frailest, had their own pet caterpillars, cooing at them and caressing them. "Wanna meet Baby Bop? This is Baby Bop and this is Barney," one of the largest, toughest sixth-grade girls proudly said, transformed, hypnotized by her own fuzzy creature. Half of the animals were smuggled back into school in sleeves, pockets, hoods, and lunch boxes.

Sand from the graffiti-removing power wash was hoarded, smoothed at the base of the school wall and used for fingers and Matchbox cars. I watched with interest to see what the children were doing with the foul-smelling material and was told, "Don't tell. They'll take it away." When a child took a broom left in a doorway and used it to sweep up debris, the broom was confiscated.

The space itself became a toy. The lone tree was a base for tag. "Not it." The stairs and stoop and the diagonal space behind it served as jail. "Tag her and she's free." Doors became sites for danger and affection, squishing friends and acquaintances into tight spots. The grates on the windows were targets for tennis balls brought from home. "I got five stuck. Can you beat me?" The demi-wall near the steps down to the gym became an obstacle over which Superman flew. "It's a bird, It's a plane, It's Richie!" The recessed back wall served as a lounge for the physically shy.[13]

Classic homemade toys could be found: paper airplanes, jump ropes made of interlocking rubber bands, homemade slam books, with pages for friends and secret codes for others. Pens became toys when used for drawing on each other's arms for April Fools' Day. Hats became balls, snagged off a target's head and chucked to third parties as far away as possible. The body itself, the original toy, reemerges when nothing else is left, inviting some kind of stimulation when doing jump rope, such as trying it barefoot—anything to heighten experience and avoid boredom.

Opportunities for touch were rare in the school day, and in the school yard, adults told children, "Put her down" or "Stop holding hands" or

"Get off him" even if the one in question was laughing and both of the participants were enjoying the activity. Games allowed friends as well as siblings and cousins to touch and engage in informal goofing. Tickling, hand holding, bear hugging, head patting, shoulder patting, clothes adjusting, hair fixing, and nose rubbing were all observed. One could say that touching games were an antidote for the scary stories in the children's brains, the same stories that spilled out into the stories of danger and the songs of the body.

Tag, the most basic game of negotiating safety and danger, rules and lawbreaking, wove among the game spaces of Sui, hopscotch, basketball, and the movable rope games. Tag used to be called "Touched Last" but now it is more like "Touch and Don't Be Caught." Mill School versions include Freeze Tag, regular tag, and Build Up, a popular new version where the child who is it holds hands with the children who are tagged, forming an enormous group. Sometimes the game dissolves into darting runs and quick touches. Snag is the stealing of a hat or scarf, the parading of it around the school yard, and its eventual return. Like young antelopes or puppies, younger children not attached to specific games would run and tap and weave new variations in old patterns of movement. These children often would run away from or circle the wide-eyed grown-ups in their midst. Grown-ups were both frames and props, with individual reputations for tolerance or hostility.

- 4 -

"NIKE, NIKE, WHO CAN DO THE NIKE?"

New Commercialization and Scripted Exploitation

At the Mill School, *rope* almost always meant double-dutch jump rope. A rich African American street tradition, rope links children to each other and to moves and phrases absorbed as common culture. Two players turn two long ropes (or one laundry line doubled over) and rhythmically rotate them eggbeater style. The jumper must skillfully leap in between as the two ropes beat their rhythm, pit pat pit pat, and execute a number of specific steps without getting tangled.

In 1991, double-dutch jump rope at the Mill School yard was a game solely for African American working-class girls. The players had Africanized names—Kenya, Aisha, and Tamika—and prided themselves on their street game repertoire. Bused in from poorer neighborhoods, these girls did not socialize much with the middle-class African American girls, most of whom had names like their white neighbors—Violet, Julie, and Claire. The game was shunned by white working-class and middle-class girls along with their middle-class African American peers. By 1999, many white European American working-class girls jumped, as did a few middle-class black girls. On most days, at least two mixed-race games emerged. Rope's increasing popularity was a convenient target for marketing campaigns.

Younger girls had to turn first, and those of really low status had "ends," the open tips of the doubled-over laundry line. "No flicking" meant turn it well, for nothing was more annoying to a skilled jumper than a turner who could not turn. If you were lucky, someone would offer you a "freebie," and you could just jump in.

> You flicked it! You got ends!
> Freebie!

Many traditional double-dutch songs list specific steps in order, and the commercial ones utilize the old formulas well:

footsies—two basic running steps with one small two-footed bounce
hopsies—one-footed hopping
bouncies—two-footed small jumps
turnsies—a complete rotation while inside the two turning ropes
walksies—basic running step
criss—crossing both legs, repeated while jumping.

At times, multiple players jump at the same time, and jumpers often improvise, adding fancy turns and gestures while increasing the speed and duration of the jumping. The game was studied by the Mill School's seven-year-olds and perfected by the twelve-year-olds. Tamika, a skilled sixth-grader, reminisced:

> I started in, like, first or second grade—got to be first or second—because I never knew how to jump. But my cousin was in, my cousin was in the eighth grade and my cous used to always play rope.

Tashi and Tamika's peers were handed new commercial rhymes that were so syncopated, so smooth in the mouth, that they were repeated word for word. These new rhymes were slick jump rope games, emerging from carefully placed ad campaigns. Some were from jump rope competitions, sponsored by the "Big Three" corporations whose names were in the jingles— Nike, Reebok, and McDonald's.

The children who jumped rope spoke these words every day, over and over, each time I observed in 1991, 1999, and 2004. Unlike earlier generations, which parodied commercials during play, the Mill School girls repeated the jingles verbatim, though the children were not robots.[1] They concentrated on moving their own way, adding fancy jumps, turns, and twists, leaning on an older tradition for variation. They parodied each other's styles, exaggerated gestures, rolled their eyes at each other, and burst out laughing. Movement offers commentary when the words make little room for it—assuming that the players are allowed to move.

This chapter introduces the new commercially scripted jump rope rhymes, which have yet to be published anywhere, and makes a case for paying attention to their increasing popularity. On the one hand, they squeeze out older, bolder, more subversively dreamy traditional rhymes; on the other hand, the children utilize traditional style and turn the advertisements into what they really are—a big game.

The games with commercial texts were consistently used to teach outsiders the African American art of double-dutch. They are the "easiest," the students said, "our favorite." "It's what you use when you don't have nothing else."

Nike	Reebok
Nike, Nike	*R-E-E*
Who can do the Nike?	*B-O-K*
Foot to the N-I-K-E	*Do your footsies, the Reebok way*
Hop to the N-I-K-E	*R-E-E*
Walk to the N-I-K-E	*B-O-K*
Bounce to the N-I-K-E	*Do your hopsies, the Reebok way*
Turn to the N-I-K-E	*R-E-E*
Criss to the N-I-K-E	*B-O-K*
(1992, 2004)	*Do your walksies, the Reebok way*
	R-E-E
	B-O-K
	Do your bouncies, the Reebok way
	R-E-E
	B-O-K
	Do your turnsies, the Reebok way
	R-E-E
	B-O-K
	Do your crissies, the Reebok way
	(1992, 2004)

Big Mac (Version 1)

Big Mac, Filet o' Fish
Quarter Pounder, Frenchie fries
Icee Coke, milk shake, foot

Filet o' Fish
Quarter Pounder, Frenchie fries
Icee Coke, milk shake, bounce

Filet o' Fish
Quarter Pounder, Frenchie fries
Icee Coke, milk shake, hop

Filet o' Fish
Quarter Pounder, Frenchie fries
Icee Coke, milk shake, turn

Filet o' Fish
Quarter Pounder, Frenchie fries
Icee Coke, milk shake, criss

Filet o' Fish
Quarter Pounder, Frenchie fries
Icee Coke, milk shake, walk
(1991, 1992, 1999, 2004)

Big Mac (Version 2)

Big Mac, Filet o' Fish, shake and fries
She's a mean mama honey and that's no lie
Together
McDonald's got footsies, play that beat
McDonald's got hopsies
(1992, 1999)

Challenge, Challenge/Big Mac/Hey Consolation Medley
(Challenge is a competitive follow-the-leader game.)

Challenge, Challenge
1, 2, 3, 4, 5, 6, 7, 8, 9, 10

Big <u>Mac</u>, Filet o' <u>Fish</u>, <u>foot</u>
And <u>bounce</u>
And <u>hop</u>
And <u>turn</u>
And <u>walk</u>
And <u>criss</u>

<u>Hey</u> consolation
<u>Where</u> have you <u>been</u>?
<u>Around</u> the <u>corner</u>, and <u>back</u> again
<u>Stole</u> my <u>money</u>
<u>Knocked</u> my <u>honey</u>
<u>Papa's</u> got the <u>hiccups</u>
<u>Mama's</u> got the <u>ice</u>
So <u>come</u> on <u>baby</u>
Let's <u>slice</u> that <u>ice</u>

2, 4, 6, 8, 10, <u>hop</u>
2, 4, 6, 8, 10, <u>turn</u>
2, 4, 6, 8, 10, <u>criss</u>
2, 4, 6, 8, 10, <u>walk</u>
(1991, 1992, 1999, 2004)[2]

Only one song mixes modern commentary, traditional moves, and commercial messages. Although it mentions specific corporations, it is not a simple advertisement. The first two lines come from a rap by recording artist KRS-One,[3] but the rest of the Mill School's version diverges from the original yet stays true to its message of confidence. Tashi and Naisha gave it special status, and its words were sung with an eye twinkle. This one was different. It is complex in its layering of street competition, sarcasm, and African American traditional footwork. In this sense, it is much more like a traditional singing game.

Criminal Minded (Version 1)

Criminal _minded_, you been _blinded_
Looking for a _shoe_ like mine, can't _find_ it

Mine costs _more_
Yours costs _less_
Mine _Footlocker_
Yours _Payless_

So _criminal minded_
Foot, you _got_ it
Criminal minded
Hop, you _got_ it
Criminal minded
Walk, you _got_ it
Criminal minded
Criss, you _got_ it
_(2004)_

Criminal Minded (Version 2)

Criminal _minded_, you been _blinded_
Looking for a _shoe_ like mine, can't _find_ it

Mine costs _more_
Yours cost _less_
Mine _Footlocker_
Yours _Payless_

Do your _footsies_, 1, 2, and 3
And your _hopsies_, 1, 2, and 3
And your _bouncies_, 1, 2, and 3
And your _walksies_, 1, 2 and 3
And your _turnsies_, 1, 2 and 3
And your _crisses_, 1, 2 and 3
_(1999)_

The original rap begins:

> *Criminal minded, you've been blinded*
> *Looking for a style like mine, you can't find it*
> *They are the audience, I am the lyricist*
> *Sometimes the suckas on the side got to hear this*
> *Page, a rage, and I'm not in a cage*
> *Free as a bird to fly up out on stage*

In a soundscape of balls bouncing against cement and against brick walls, children screaming "Not it," and whistles blowing, "Nike, Nike," "Big Mac," and "Reebok" rose above the din in the Mill School yard— "Nike, Nike" hollered against the wall, "Reebok" hooted near the hopscotch, "Big Mac" shouted in the middle of the yard. On some days, they were the only words sung. Even when children were waiting their turn, there was an audible low rumble of "Big, Mac, Filet o' Fish, Quarter Pounder, Frenchie fries, icee Coke, milk shake, foot, Filet o' Fish, Quarter Pounder, Frenchie fries . . ." Throughout the 1990s and into the 2000s, the commercial text remained number 1.

Each audiotape and each videotape and every page of field notes were placed in a spreadsheet of games played, sorted by genre and game title. If girls in multiple ropes were singing the same song, I counted it only once. Recordings (singing or commentary) were then transcribed. I eventually shared the videos with the players and transcribed their comments. Commentary focused on skill and performance style, an emic, or inside, perspective that clarified group dynamics but not the big picture. Getting a sense of that picture requires numbers.

In 1992, twenty-three of the fifty-six rope rhymes performed (41 percent) had commercial themes; in 1999, that figure had risen to twenty-six of thirty-eight (68 percent). The shrinking remainder, from 60 percent to 30 percent, included all the older traditional rhymes. "Big Mac" was heard daily from 1991 through 1999 and into 2004, while "Reebok" and "Nike" gradually made their way into the mainstream rope repertoire. I was shocked not only by their prevalence but by their dramatic increase over time. Rope was not more popular in 1999—there were always several games going on simultaneously. The commercial texts were now more popular.

The commercial texts became new bridges between neighborhoods, social classes, and ethnicities. If the movement was taken away, however, the shouting was reduced to a monotonous mumble, and the fire left the girls' eyes. I could not help but picture the singers in McDonald's uniforms, like their high school cousins who worked at the Mickey Dee up the street. Big Mac, Filet o' Fish, Next Please.

These commercial rhymes are also qualitatively different from the commercial parodies of the 1970s:

> McDonald's is our kind of place
> They feed you rattlesnakes
> Hamburgers up your nose
> French fries between your toes
> The next time that you go there
> They'll steal your underwear
> McDonald's is our kind of place[4]

> McDonald's is your kind of place
> Hamburgers in your face
> French fries up your nose
> Ketchup between your toes
> McDonald's is your kind of place
> Ain't got no parking space
> McDonald's is your kind of place[5]

> Winston tastes good like a cigarette should
> No filter, no taste, just a fifty cent waste[6]

> Winston tastes bad like the last one I had
> No filter, no flavor, just plain toilet paper[7]

> Oh! I wish I wasn't an Oscar Meyer Wiener
> That is what I wouldn't want to be
> Because if I was an Oscar Meyer Wiener
> There would soon be nothin' left of me.[8]

We do not know anything about how frequent these earlier rhymes were sung. We only know they were interesting, like the objects in Grandmother's attic. But some collections are more than merely interesting, possessing historical weight and significance. They are part of a particular generation's treasure chest.

Sociologist Pierre Bourdieu reminds us that "this space of sports is not a universe closed in on itself. It is inserted into a system of practices and consumptions themselves structured and constituted as a system. We are altogether justified in treating sporting practices as a relatively autonomous space, but you shouldn't forget that this space is a locus of forces which do not apply only to it."[9] Given the volume of commercial messages presented to children via television and radio, on billboards and storefronts, on clothing and food items, it is not surprising to find commercial texts increasingly prevalent in children's lore. But this phenomenon represents more than just a repository of larger cultural images. Some commercials are emerging right in the school's classroom.

Channel 1 is the commercially driven television show that advertises directly in classrooms on a daily basis. The well-publicized deal allows poor schools across the country gain access to free media technology in exchange for permitting students to view advertising in the classroom.[10] Every class in the Mill School had a television monitor provided by Channel 1, and every morning Channel 1's "news" and "entertainment" shows could be heard drifting down the hallway. The commercial songs in the school yard are reinforced not only by the commercial breaks between segments of shows but by the characters in the educational programs: "I sure could go for a cheeseburger," said the story's happy lion. The fourth-graders take in everything—story, burger, and bun.

The terms of the Mill School's contract with Channel 1 required administrators to play the commercially sponsored "educational" program every school day. No matter how large the generosity of Channel 1, the Ronald McDonald House, or Nike's Project PLAY (a $10 million sport and playground program), the agenda is to fill children's bodies with a McDonald's-approved diet and cover them with Nike-approved footwear.[11] These acts of charity can be seen as at best assuaging corporate guilt and at worst as image manipulation.

McDonald's representatives confirmed to me that the Big Mac chant had arisen from a campaign conducted in the advertising inserts included with Sunday newspapers. I received a copy of the record, which was designed to look like a jukebox and presented the "menu chant" version as a mock lesson:

> Good Morning, Class.
> Today we're going to learn the McDonald's Menu Song and give a listener out there a chance to win a million dollars. So repeat after me: Big Mac, Filet o' Fish . . .

At the end of the recording, nobody wins. Only the teacher can properly say the Big Mac rhyme.

McDonald's, Reebok, and Nike each sponsor national double-dutch competitions. Coaches of local double-dutch leagues long for corporate sponsorship of their underfunded community programs. The corporate sponsorship supports the double-dutch leagues, which in their professionalism require uniforms and sneakers. And this corporate largesse comes with corporate jingles.

But these campaigns ask poor children to purchase what they cannot afford. Black children, who make up the majority of Philadelphia's poor and the majority of the Mill School's student body, are doubly exploited; poor, black, female children are triply exploited.[12] In an environment where raw materials are inaccessible and are consistently removed from playtime, poorer African American children, heirs to their neighborhoods' rich oral and movement traditions, are teaching non–African Americans what can be done, as Naisha said, "when you don't have nothing else."

The literature, as Paul Willis has suggested, alternates between salivation and disgust: Vanderbilt glibly writes, "Every three months, Nike introduces a dozen new basketball shoes, and it has become standard industry procedure for marketing and design staff to visit Philadelphia, Chicago, and New York with bags of samples to get reactions from the kids. . . . We go to the playground, and we just dump the shoes out. It's unbelievable. The kids go nuts. That's when you realize the importance of Nike. Having kids tell you Nike is the number one thing in their life— number two is their girlfriend."[13] Goldman and Papson offer, "Think of the Nike swoosh like a piggy bank. Every time you watch a Nike ad that gives you viewing pleasure, or provides a moment of identification, or that encourages you to think of Nike as committed to something broader than its own self-interest, then you deposit a little bit of value (almost like dropping a coin in the piggy bank) into the sign. . . . Relying on the swoosh to brand its business has paid off handsomely in an annual growth rate of roughly 40 percent in the mid '90s."[14]

The Mill School's fourth-grade boys bounce up and down in their chairs when they talk about basketball:

> We play basketball more than we play any other sport
> *We beat Room 4—*
> **Like eight times.**
> *We blew Room 5 twenty-two times.*
> It's basketball season right now, [and on the court you hear]—
> *"You got Reebok Walkers?"*

In light of the recognition that comes with sound and motion, each sneaker conversation and each jump rope jingle is money in the bank for Nike, McDonald's, or Reebok. Like the Coca-Cola logo painted on the bottom of Philadelphia's public swimming pools and stenciled onto the backboards of recreation center basketball hoops, the school yard becomes a television screen for an agenda that is not that of the children or the school and that benefits no one in the school region with a livable wage. The corporation buys the children's time, which the school, in turn, squeezes.

Argun Appadurai refers to the mixing of tradition and commercialism as "the double inversion" of nostalgia and progressive greed, "a recurring rhetorical strategy" among advertisers.[15] The mixing "might be regarded as the critical cultural move of advanced capitalism."[16] It is a doubly inverted looping of culturally sanctioned commercial texts playing off game patterns by age, race, ethnicity, gender, and class. Commercial games have become a new tradition, simultaneously old and brand-new, that is embedded in the folkloric process of cultural recycling and fueled by industry.

Hip-hop, rope's older male cousin, is itself ambiguous, a mix of rebellion and consumption, caught between subculture and escape route from that subculture. Cornell West writes, "Although hip-hop culture has become tainted by the very excesses and amorality it was born in rage against, the best of rap music and hip-hop culture still expresses stronger and more clearly than any cultural expression in the past generation a profound indictment of the moral decadence of our dominant society."[17]

Like jazz before them, hip-hop and school yard rhymes are misunderstood, unappreciated, and eaten up by racialized commercial interests beyond their control.[18] Sociologist Juliet Schor takes us further: "Although many aspects of African American culture have had a long historical association with cool, such as jazz and sartorial styles, as well as a legacy of contributions to popular culture, what is happening now is unique. Never before have inner-city styles and cultural practices been such a dominant influence on, even a definer of, popular culture. . . . [I]n the words of Douglas Holt again . . . it is now the context itself—the neighborhood, the pain of being poor, the alienation experience of black kids. These are the commodifiable assets."[19]

But Naisha and Tashi have their own list of commodifiable assets. They require that a song be aesthetically pleasing, that it have an interesting rhythm, that it be familiar enough that it is immediately obvious what to do, that it allow for skill—serious skill—to be displayed, and that it be fast. They can mix and match movement styles with prefabricated texts, and if they have the freedom, they can make medleys all their own—"Big Mac" with "Hey Consolation," "Nike" with "Big Fat Stick."

West's words offer not only critique but also wisdom: "The genius of our black foremothers and forefathers was to create powerful buffers to ward off the nihilistic threat, to equip black folk with cultural armor to beat back the demons of hopelessness, meaninglessness, and lovelessness. . . . But why this shattering of black civil society, this weakening of black cultural institutions in asphalt jungles? Corporate market institutions have contributed greatly to this situation."[20] Tamika says, "We learn songs, like, when, like, our mothers, like, they learned from their mothers. We learned from them." Drawing strength from their mothers, sisters, and cousins, the children intuitively face the incoming commercial scripting and focus on the variability of their moves as their words become script.

When asked where "Big Mac" originated, the children unanimously respond by singing, "Big Mac, Filet o' Fish, Quarter Pounder Frenchie fries, icee Coke, milk shake, foot." Shaniya offered, "I would see it like up at McDonald's." They continue, "Filet o' Fish, Quarter Pounder, Frenchie fries, icee Coke, milk shake, hop." Without realizing what they are saying, the children repeat the words and enjoy the cleverness of the rhythm and turn their attention to what they can control, their bodies, and focus on them while negotiating with peers.

Aisha instructs her Polish American classmate where to enter the ropes and compromises, allowing the jumper to begin in the middle of the unmoving ropes. Starting that way looks easier, the girls tell me as they watch themselves on video, but it is not. They say that the best way is to enter near the turner and catch the wave of the turning line when one rope is at its top and the other is at its bottom. Stay close together, don't put yourself in the middle of things. "Big Mac" and "Nike" are the easiest chants, they explain, although the list of steps is no different than many of the traditional rhymes. They mean that the commercial texts are culturally the easiest, the most recognizable, the most frequently heard. When Tammy misses, the onlookers shout, "Saved by all," while other observers giggle and practice their footwork without the turning ropes, their freedom of movement serving as a cultural editing process. Aisha looks critically at Tammy's footwork and raises a hand in instruction. Naisha invites Tammy to follow along, lifting her feet lightly, left, right, left, right: "Do it again. 'Big Mac, Filet o' Fish.'"

- 5 -

RESTRICTED MOVEMENT IN A SCRIPTED WORLD

The school yard is tense at times: "They always beat us [to the door]." "I'm first, first." "Second!" "What time is it? Third!" "Aw, I'm gonna be last." "You got to call it." "You got to call it quick."

First!
Second!
Places erases!
No, reverse it down.
Ace, ace, first, second.
Ace, ace, got no higher.
I called it.
She called it.
Ace, ace.
Yes, she did.

The tension and the race to play are most visible at the times of transition, between the ringing of the bell and the reentry to school. As the frames push and pull, the children sneak some joy in the short time allowed—in their movement, in each other's company, in rhythm, parody, and synchrony. In a very palpable sense, a piece of the playground becomes a battlefield, as the parties fight over cultural capital, superimposed on the daily battle of fair and foul, it and not it.

Frantic to avoid being interrupted, children shout, "Don't be stopping us. We're playin' here." Basketball players literally hold onto the post to claim their position; boys ready themselves for the next game, dribbling balls long past the bell. Most try to keep playing. Some are more graceful than others.

A boy stalls and keeps playing football as one of the female aides yells at him to stop. The adults threaten to take away the football. At the last possible moment, the boy does a touchdown dance, little steps to the right and left, pumps his fist, does a slippery back bend, and then spikes the football. Only then is he ready to come in, and he does so cheerfully. The tug-of-war, invented by the grown-ups, disappears.

To see the complexity of the connections among cultural scripts, children's subculture, use of games as negotiating tools, and the institution of school itself requires an analysis of the most dramatic themes shown by the transcriptions of the videotapes. This analysis allows us to see, frame by frame, how the children are pulled as they negotiate.

In this chapter, I analyze videotapes of the "Big Mac" rhyme. I focus not on the production of Big Macs but on the swift-footed delivery of commercial icons into popular culture. The clips include an advanced double-dutch session, a single rope session done in double-dutch style, a single rope session done in single rope style, and a double-dutch lesson for girls who had never before played this style.

Video Clip 1

Time	Action	Voice
10:45:10	Aisha prepares to enter ropes; she pushes a boy out of the way.	
10:45:17	Aisha jumps.	Big Mac, Filet o' Fish
10:45:20	She misses. Young spectator laughs. Both Aisha and Kenya gesture as if to enter the rope.	
10:45:30	Aisha jumps in again, does fancy turns while doing basic steps.	Big Mac, Filet o' Fish, Quarter Pounder, Frenchie fries, icee Coke, milk shake, hop
10:45:40	Aisha misses. Rica parodies her style. They laugh.	
10:45:45	Kenya and Rica prepare. Rica enters rope.	Big Mac, Filet o' Fish
	Rica misses.	
10:45:58	Aisha enters and misses. They move closer to the building.	"Shade child. Shade honey, shade." "Turn it around I know you hate turning that thing [the camera] around, and I don't blame you."

	[Camera rotates]	"I'd follow you guys anywhere."
10:46:19	Kenya enters rope.	Big Mac, Filet o' Fish, Quarter Pounder, Frenchie fries
10:46: 25	Kenya misses, whips rope off.	

Aisha added an extra challenge and performed her whole sequence while turning. Rica followed the challenge, but Kenya did not. They parody each other's styles and chat while chanting.

Video Clip 2

Time	Action	Voice
10:39:09	Joy jumps a single rope that is turned by two others; Fria mumbles "Big Mac" on the side.	Big Mac, Filet o' Fish, Quarter Pounder, Frenchie fries, icee Coke, milk shake, bounce, Big Mac, Filet o' Fish, Quarter Pounder, Frenchie fries, icee Coke, milk shake, hop, Big Mac, Filet o' Fish, Quarter Pounder, Frenchie fries, icee Coke, milk shake, turn, Big Mac, Filet o' Fish, Quarter Pounder, Frenchie fries, icee Coke, milk shake, criss, Big Mac, Filet o' Fish, Quarter Pounder, Frenchie fries, icee Coke, milk shake.
10:39:27	Boy interrupts.	YAH!
	Joy pushes him out and Coco, an older girl, puts an arm around Joy and brings her back to the game.	
10:39:33	Child who is not playing comments.	The bell's gonna ring in five minutes.
10:39:36	Fria jumps in and sings to herself.	Big Mac, Filet o' Fish, Quarter Pounder, Frenchie fries, icee Coke, milk shake, foot, Big Mac, Filet o' Fish, Quarter Pounder, Frenchie fries, icee Coke, milk shake, hop.
	Child who is not playing comments.	"Good. I'm freezing."
	Fria is not really hopping.	
10:39:49	Joy shouts.	Hop! Hop! Filet o' Fish hop hop hop
	Coco joins in, singing.	Filet o' Fish, Quarter Pounder, icee Coke, milk shake, turn.
10:39:55	Joy and Coco do motions in place.	Big Mac, Filet o' Fish, Quarter Pounder, icee Coke, milk shake, criss.
10:40:05	Fria misses, dances in place.	You got her ends.

Joy and Fria chant "Big Mac" while managing interruptions. When Fria begins to lose her energy and repeat "Big Mac" in a monotone drone, Joy shouts, "Hop, hop, hop" and demands that Fria reinvigorate her steps. The game's rules require the girls' continued attentiveness. They watch over each other and make sure that their bodies stay alert. They are also hyperaware of the passing time, even though they are not wearing watches. These two clips point to the variability of the body motions and the uses of the larger rope tradition to keep the action moving, together, and light.

Video Clip 3

Time	Action	Voice
10:40:15	Queenie jumps single rope, two girls turning. She jumps with both feet, not double-dutch style. All three girls are African American.	[Silence.]
10:40:27	Queenie misses. Randy, a European American, jumps in.	
10:40:29	A second girl, Vicky, jumps in with Randy. They stop.	No, no, no.
10:40:36	They jump together, facing each other.	[Laughter.]
10:40:38	Randy tries again, misses.	Hey, come on!
10:40:43	They switch. Sheena enters the rope alone.	
10:40:51	Sings to herself.	Quarter Pounder, Frenchie fries, icee Coke, milk shake, foot
10:41:02	School bell rings. Vicky jumps in. Aliah, who is turning, yells; S gets mad, jumps again.	Bell rings again; child screams. No, don't jump in.
		Quarter Pounder, Frenchie fries, icee Coke, milk shake, turn, Quarter Pounder, Frenchie fries, icee Coke, milk shake, criss
10:41:17	Vicky jumps in with Sheena; they miss. Sheena gets mad. Randy tries to collect the rope.	

Here, the bell changes everything. The two-person jumping shifts from giddy to grumpy. The girls jump after the bell rings, and the session ends when the jumper is interrupted by another attempt at two-person jumping. The clip is unusual in its mix of single rope and double-dutch styles and its inclusions of white and black girls jumping together.

Video Clip 4

Time	Action	Voice
10:46:50	Kim, a Chinese immigrant, is trying to learn double-dutch.	Big Mac, Filet o' Fish.
	She misses.	
10:47:01	A younger, second-grade girl turns to her audience and points.	Saved! Saved!
	The younger girls dance in place.	
10:47:05	Anya, a Polish American sixth-grader, enters the rope. She is told nonverbally to lift her feet. The lead turner, a sixth-grade African American girl, checks to see which foot is lifted and coordinates the turning as the other girl stands in the middle of the rope.	
10:47:12		One, two, three.
10:47:15	The jumper runs in place and gets tangled. The lead turner coordinates with the girl who has ends to lift at the same time.	
10:47:20	The jumper jumps high, both feet together, and misses.	Big Mac. I told you not to come down.
10:47:27	School bell rings.	
	Little girls jump up and down. A nearby boy jumps in front of the camera and shakes his body violently. Kim gets knocked over and begins to cry.	

Clips 3 and 4 show a desperation to keep playing, and the most stressed moment is when play is interrupted by the bell. The sound literally shocks the players' bodies and seems to be correlated with anger and potential violence. However, as I have demonstrated, recess is not violent at the Mill School—the transitions are. The hardest moments are when commercial power meets the institutional power of school. This intersection represents a larger problem of consumption and restriction. What will happen when the rebellion of the body can no longer shake off Nike or sneak away from the Big Fat Stick? What happens when play or motion is severely limited?

Susie and Naisha sneak food in their classroom, passing it around to share like contraband. Malik and Mikee throw away their uneaten lunches to play their favorite games. The hopscotch girls choose to eat only when they are delegated to the passive role of not playing. Donna and Sheryl play the game of not eating and are slumped against the wall outside. Bobby moans, "There just isn't time to enough to eat and play. . . . By the time I get my school lunch, it's over." The situation is a conflict inside conflicts, the body and its support system versus the culture of consumption and the rules of the school.

I marvel at how "Nike" and "Big Fat Stick," commercialism and school control, both pull against and reinforce each other. In the school yard, these two profoundly influential forces are strong, especially at times of transition. As shaped by patterns of gender, race, and class, the desire to play and consume more play is yanked by the grown-ups in charge. According to sociologist Daniel Bell,[1] such contrasting forces show the conflict between the technical machinery that supports the economy and the conservative pull of culture. Yet here it is the opposite. The technical machinery of both schooling and the economy conserve the status quo, while the culture of urban childhood innovates through its well-preserved traditions. In many ways, keeping working-class children passive suits the larger culture just fine. Rather, the intention of schooling and the machinery of schooling conflict.

The real recess problem is an education problem in disguise. Do schools want children to take risks, enjoy leadership, struggle with justice, and be creative, or are working-class schools really just preparing "working-class kids for working-class jobs"?[2] In his most recent lamentation about American education, Jonathan Kozol (2005) describes the "shame of the nation" and the horrendous economic and racial inequities that exist in schools.[3] He suggests the need for a "misery index" to describe just how oppressive schools are. Is it the function of schools to make children miserable and to make poor children, especially those of color, the most miserable of all?

Sigmund Freud saw the civilizing process as antithetical to the pursuit of happiness: "What do they demand of life and wish to achieve in it? The answer to this can hardly be in doubt. They strive after happiness; they want to become happy and remain so . . . and yet its program is at loggerheads with the whole world, with the macrocosm as with the microcosm."[4]

In the most telling book on class differences in child development, Annette Lareau writes that the opportunities denied to poor children are ameliorated by their relative freedom and their opportunities to connect to each other.[5] The Mill School and similar institutions attempt to remove those freedoms without the gains available at upper-middle-class schools. In short, at school and on the playground, these children are being squeezed as they are being groomed for boring, miserable career options. They hear that this and that are forbidden and "Big Mac, Filet o' Fish," and they have to make do with ever-decreasing opportunities to tell it like it is.

Schooling does not have to take place at the expense of happiness, although it appears to be moving in that direction nationally. According to one parent advocating for her child, "My 6 year old has her only recess of the day taken away from her 3 times in week because she did not complete morning work one day, she asked to borrow a marker from her neighbor in class (as they are not allowed to borrow or share, 1st grade), and must have gotten mixed up about having 'lunch detention' and told the lunchroom monitor she did not have it so she had to serve a third because she 'LIED.' Is this appalling or what?"[6]

Another parent complains, "My son's class is to lose 7 days of recess, everyone! Because some of the students were yelling when the office called up to the classroom—the teacher was not in the room. Why should they all be punished and why use something as important as recess. The teacher would not change his mind on the punishment so my husband and I are going to meet with the principal. If they will not change their stance on the punishment I will go to the school each of those days and take my son out for lunch and recess then return him to class. What else can I do when something is unjust but I have no power?"

In February 2004, Texas parent Sandy Buckalew asked for advice: "I have worked hard to persuade our school district not to drop recess, especially in elementary school. My efforts have been unsuccessful and they have all but eliminated daily recess here in our city. My son, age 8, has attended the same school since kindergarten, and until this year had enjoyed 2 daily recesses. Now with the mandated P.E. hours in public schools our district has dropped recess to 2 ten-minute breaks per week. That's right! 20 mins. of recess for the whole week. . . . I see too much of 'If it's not problematic in my home, right now, then I won't get involved.' Problem is . . . they don't see the bigger picture. How are these youngsters to release their energy? Exercise their imaginations? Or pick up those important tools for social development?"[7]

Many parents are embittered by the lack of official response, although some progress has occurred. Michigan and Virginia now have policies mandating recess. Texas teachers must have a "good reason" to deny children their recess time. But is testing a "good reason"? Is "enrichment" a good reason? "Maintenance of school control"? Everywhere I have lectured on the subject, people have told me their recess stories in hushed tones and urgent whispers. At academic conferences on education, anthropology, and folklore, teachers, administrators, and parents always have the same reaction: an initial chuckle at the seemingly trivial subject and then an urgent telling of tales of their own children, their siblings' children, their neighbors' children who are stressed, overprogrammed, or understimulated and have almost no time to play.

In Chicago, I was told about "silent lunches," where children are prohibited not only from playing but even from talking as they eat. In Massachusetts, I heard about children who were considered bright and were encouraged by their teachers to forgo the playground in favor of extra instruction during the twenty-minute lunch break. In Florida, some elementary school children have recess only once a week. In the wealthier Philadelphia suburbs, I learned of children losing recess for enrichment, testing, and advanced work. Everywhere, parents worried about their slow eaters being rushed, encouraged to sacrifice basic physical comfort for the sake of school and at the expense of play. "Can you talk to my son's teacher? My principal? Write the book for them."

Bjorn Grinde suggests that we are creatures whose happiness and ability to thrive are easily disrupted when we are placed in an environment that does not allow us to do what we need to do.[8] Children wishing to play are doing what children have done for eons, integrating their individual worlds with the worlds around them, synthesizing what Erik Erikson has called "the bodily and social processes with the self."[9]

The new field of positive psychology suggests what Tashi and Lilly and Eddie and Darnell have always known: When you make yourself happier, the world is easier to tolerate.[10] But to see the struggle for happiness without the seemingly arbitrary causes for pain is to blame the victim for not being jubilant enough.

When the children saw themselves on tape, they giggled, laughed, and guffawed at each other's antics and noted how their bodies had changed. Eager, almost desperate to tell their recess stories, they asked to come back for more.

I want to see the tapes, I want to see all the tapes.
(I wish we could, but we're out of time. But is there anything else that any-
body wants to say?)
Ooh.
Me.
Can we come back here at lunch?

Students inevitably requested permission to show me one more game,
to sing one more song into the microphone. One shy girl looked up at
me after doing her last hand clap and sighed, "There's so much stuff I
want to say." When I told her to go ahead and say it, she sighed again:
"My name [sighing, with a whoosh of rushed air]—my name's Aisha."
Cheeks flushed with the excitement of speaking about things that matter, the students proceed down the hallway with me. Gina, a gymnast,
does a cartwheel. Two others imitate her; they are bursting with energy,
doing flips, cartwheels, not making a sound. The building's manager
stops them in the middle of the hallway and says, "Are you nuts or
something? What's the matter with you?"

Social theorist and historian Michel Foucault has written of the body
and its ultimate control in the prison, a metaphor often heard when children describe school—the bars on the windows, the rules, the extreme
time limitations, the barking directives.[11] He describes the "micro-phys-
ics of power" among French prisoners in 1837: "There is recreation until
twenty minutes to eleven. . . . At twenty minutes to one, [they] leave
the school, and return to their courtyards for recreation. At five minutes
to one, at the drum-roll, they form into work teams." Even prisoners
had recess twice a day. Presaging Pierre Bourdieu and Foucault, Charles
Dickens noted that the institutions of power—jails, hospitals, schools—
were practically indistinguishable in working-class communities, where
the movement of the body was proscribed.[12] Then and now, the playful
social body offers escape, but now the words are increasingly scripted.
What can we learn about human adaptation and creativity as children's
movement is restricted in a scripted world? At what point does research
evolve into advocacy?

Part 3

PLAY AND CHILDREN'S CULTURE

Jump rope

- 6 -

"WORK THAT BODY, ODDY, ODDY"

Lessons from "Old School" Rhymes

Traditions serve as a form of advocacy. In 2004, Tashi eyed me with her brown doe eyes, stood up a little taller, and marked her steps in place as she sang her favorite rope games without a rope: the one the school provided was too short, too stiff, and unusable for double-dutch. She sang loudly and strongly: "Big Mac," "Nike," and "Eedie, Idie Odie, Here Comes the Teacher with a Big Fat Stick." "What else is sung now?" I asked. "Do you know the ones the older kids used to sing?"

Pac Man

Pac man came on tardy
And Toya had a party
She gonna move her feet
Yeah, yeah
And dance to the beat
Yeah, yeah
She gonna hop til she drop
Yeah, yeah
She gonna turn til she burn
Yeah, yeah
And criss til she miss
Yeah, yeah
(2004)

Double-dutch songs have always been about the body and have served as a hybrid changing form, in between the games of girlhood and the more sophisticated shakes of the teenage dance floor. "Turn til she burn, criss til she miss; Do the MC Hammer; Hey DJ, let's sing that song; I can do the hoochie-coochie; I can do the split; Betcha five dollars you can't do this."

Girl Scout, Girl Scout

Girl Scout, Girl Scout
Do your duty
'Cause you got a thing
And that's all that
Salute to the captain
Bow to the king
Turn all around like a submarine
Oh, I can do the hoochie-coochie
I can do the split
Bet you five dollars
You can't do this
Lady on one foot
Lady on two foot
Close your eyes and count to ten
If you miss you got too tense
1, 2, 3, 4, 5 . . .
(1992, 1999)[1]

Tashi reminded me of Rickie, some five years earlier, who had the same confidence, the same pride in repertoire. Rickie, tall and lean with long straightened hair, was a clear athlete and an acknowledged leader of the rope games. Seven years before Rickie, Naisha, too, had had that swagger; she was her generation's authority on clothes, moves, and what to sing. The three embodied leadership in this realm of the playground: knowledge, strength, and grace.

Rickie always began with "Big Mac," but "old school" rhymes would emerge on occasion, a mix of pop cultural icons and traditional style. Many are recorded for the first time here.

Boom Boom Tangle

Boom, boom, tangle
Tang, boom, tang
Yo Kenya [jumper's name], yo
Let me see you do the
MC Hammer, she said
Boom, boom, tangle
Tang, boom, tang
Boom, boom, tangle
Tang, boom, tang

Yo Kenya, yo
Let me see you do the
Bobby Brown, she said
Boom, boom, tangle
Tang, boom, tang
Boom, boom, tangle
Tang, boom, tang

Yo Kenya, yo
Let me see you do the
Heavy D, she said
Boom, boom, tangle
Tang, boom tang
Boom, boom, tangle
Tang, boom, tang

Yo Kenya, yo
Let me see you do the
Bobby Brown, she said
Boom, boom, tangle
Tang, boom, tang
Boom, boom, tangle
Tang, boom, tang

Yo Kenya, yo
Let me see you do the

Roger Rabbit, she said
Boom, boom, *tangle*
Tang, boom, *tang*
Boom, boom, *tangle*
Tang, boom, *tang*

Yo Kenya, yo
Let me *see* you *do* the
Butterfly, she said
Boom, boom, *tangle*
Tang, boom, *tang*
Boom, boom, *tangle*
Tang, boom, *tang*

Yo Kenya, yo
Let me *see* you *do* the
Honky tonk, she said
Boom, boom, *tangle*
Tang, boom, *tang*
Boom, boom, *tangle*
Tang, boom, *tang*
(1992, 1999)

When an artist's name was sung—MC Hammer, Bobby Brown, Heavy D—the girls imitated that artist's style, his moves, his gestures. The artists are mixed in with a reference to a movie character, Roger Rabbit, and the butterfly, a creature famous for its own changing body.

All the Boys

All the *boys* and *girls*
Do the *hoochie*-coochie *dance*
And the *way* they *shake*
Is *enough* to *kill* a *snake*

I *lead* shoulders *baby,* 1, 2, and 3
Head shoulders, *head* shoulders, *head* shoulders

Knee ankle baby, 1, 2, and 3
Knee ankle, knee ankle, knee ankle
Kick the bucket baby, 1, 2, and 3
(1999)[2]

Between games and sometimes while just walking around, the girls would murmur, "Knee ankle baby, 1, 2, and 3, Knee ankle baby . . ." The aesthetic was kinetic, narrative, and sometimes just for pure sound fun. They loved singing "Butt Like Mine," too, and marched around singing softly, "Beep, beep, beep," "She's all that," and giggling.

Butt Like Mine

She had a butt like mine
You know she looked so fine
And when she crossed the street
The cars go beep, beep, beep
And footsies, beep, beep, beep
And bouncies, beep, beep, beep
And hopsies, beep, beep, beep
And turnsies, beep, beep, beep
(1999)

Mini Skirt

Look at the girl with the mini skirt
You mess with her
Get your feelings hurt
She knows karate
From the front to the back
Foot, she's all that
Hop, she's all that
Bounce, she's all that
(1999)

D-I-S-H Choice

D-I-S-H choice, do your footsies
D-I-S-H choice, up the ladder
D-I-S-H choice, do your hopsies
D-I-S-H choice, round the corner
D-I-S-H choice, do your turnsies
1, 2, and 3, and a 1, 2, and 3
Hop 1, 2, and 3
Jump 1, 2 and 3
[At "choice," the jumper can do "whatever she wants".]
(1992, 1999)[3]

Hey DJ

Hey DJ let's sing that song
Keep a footin'
All night long
Hey DJ let's sing that song
Keep a hoppin'
All night long
Hey DJ let's sing that song
Keep a turnin'
All night long
Hey DJ let's sing that song
Keep a clappin'
All night long
(1992)

The body had to show endurance "all night long," and it had to show style and "get loose." Jumpers had to be disciplined ("on time") and flexible ("do it right").

Boots

Juice, juice, gotta get loose
We came here to knock some boots
Foot, oh yeah oh yeah
Hop, oh yeah oh yeah
BOUNCE, oh yeah oh yeah
(1992)

Kitty Kat Bar

Kitty kat bar
Gonna be on time
'Cause the school bell rings
At a quarter to nine
Don't be late
At a quarter to eight
1, 2, 3, oh 9
Late, late, late, late
1, 2, 3, oh 9
[Repeat until a jumper enters the rope.]
(1992)[4]

The games conserve the style, the order of the steps, and the ritual of jumping while changing and hybridizing the texts. Tashi, Rickie, and Naisha repeated their rhymes word for word but listened for better, cleverer creations, adding extra turns and fancy spins, and even jumping two at a time, editing as they went. William Wells Newell, a collector of American games at the turn of the twentieth century, noted the paradox inherent in children's culture: children are simultaneously inventive and conservative, as the next four rhymes clearly demonstrate.[5]

Bartman

*Bart*man *Bart*man
Who can *do* the *Bart*man
Foot to the B-A-R-T
Jump to the B-A-R-T
(1992)

"Do the Bartman" was a song that appeared on the television show *The Simpsons* in 1990.

Jack Be Nimble

Jack be *nimble*
Jack be *quick*
Jack hoofed up *over* a *candlestick*
Foot, hop, around the *side*
Uh huh, that *girl* from
North Philly
She *don't* take no *stuff*
From *nobody*
She's *up,* she's *down*
She's *all* around.
(1992)

Helicopter, Helicopter

*Heli*copter *Heli*copter
Please come *down*
If you *don't*
I'll *shoot* you *down*
Boom boom boom
(1999)

'N Sync, 'N Sync

'N Sync, 'N Sync
Please come down
If you don't
I'll kiss you down
Boom boom boom
(1999)

For "Helicopter" and "'N Sync," one player twirls a rope in a circle close to the ground and the other players jump over it. Not a double-dutch game, it was popular among younger girls who had not quite mastered the skill of jumping the double ropes. 'N Sync was a particularly hot boy band of the 1990s. It was not clear whether this invented version was included as a regular game or was just the musing of a dreamy girl fan.

HAND CLAPS/NUMBERS

White European American girls hardly ever participated in jump rope beyond the newest rhymes with their commercial scripts. When these girls did jump rope, it was to the "Big Mac" rhyme with a single rope, done individually. More typically, individual rope was done to numbers, counting the number of jumps (101, 102, 103). Lone European American girls could often be heard skippity-skipping around the perimeter of the school yard mumbling numbers: 203, 204 . . .

The same held true for hand clapping. In general, white girls played Silent Numbers. The classic pattern:

- clap hands, cross and clap partner's right
- clap hands, cross and clap partner's left
- clap, clap, flip hands and pat, flip front and pat
- clap pat, clap pat, clap clap, flip pat

The girls counted the claps—numbered them—and repeated the pattern: one, two, three, four, five, six, seven, eight.

White girls occasionally would join their African American classmates and do numbers that had actual songs. These songs did not involve counting but were sung to rock and roll music, southern circle games, or new versions of old jump rope rhymes made sexier. Rock and roll, itself a meeting ground for African and European traditions, provided the most popular background for a handful of games that were played dozens of times in the Mill School yard.

The texts instruct the body and ask it to move in specific ways, in a sense turning rock and roll into folk dance music. "Play that Funky Music White Boy," a hit recorded by Wild Cherry in 1978, was mixed with "Rockin' Robin," originally recorded by Bobby Day in 1958 and rerecorded by the Jackson 5. The children performed medleys, mixing rock and roll with circle game classics such as "Down by the Banks of the Hanky Pank," a game with origins in the 1890s.[6] No matter how they were mixed, these revised numbers rooted in cheers and jump rope rhymes were lighthearted, giggly events. All celebrated or poked fun at the body. Most had accented claps on the second beat, jazzing up the dominant downbeat and making the rock and roll hand claps less like singsong and more like funk.

Play that Funky Music

Words	Basic Motion (repeat for each line)
Play that funky music, white boy	clap, pat, clap, pat, clap, clap, flip, pat

Say what, Say what

Play that funky music, right
Say what, Say what

When I say rock, you say roll
When I say disco, you say soul
When I say honey, you say sweet
When I say disco, you say beat
Rock, roll
Disco, soul
Honey, sweet
Disco, beat
(1992)

Swing, Swing, Swing (or Rockin' Robin)
(foursome)

Words	Basic Motion
Swing, swing, swing	swing held hands around the circle
To the rhythm of the beat	
Hey hey	
Rockin' in the tree tops	tap side partner's hands, then clap, repeat to opposite side, clap
All night long	tap high across, opposite, clap, low across, clap, as bridges
Rockin' and a boppin' and	repeat tap and bridge pattern
All the little birdies	repeat pattern from first stanza

On *Jay*bird *Street*
Love to *hear* the *robin* go
Tweet tweet *tweet*

Rockin' Robin
Tweet, tweedle, deet
Rockin' Robin
Tweet, tweedle-ee *deet*
Oh rockin' *robin* we're
Really gonna *rock* it *tonight*
(1992, 1999)[7]

"Roaches" and "Boogers" at times were added on:

Roaches

Words	Basic Motion
I woke up Saturday morning	clap, pat, clap, pat, clap twice, flip, pat

I *woke* up by the *wall*
I *saw* a *bunch* of *roaches*
Playing basket*ball*
The *score* was *seven* to *nothing*
They *got* that *game beat*
I *got* my *can* of *roach* spray
And sprayed 1, 2, 3
(1999)[8]

Boogers

Words
Mama's in the kitchen

Basic Motion
clap, pat, clap, pat, clap twice, flip, pat

Daddy's in the hall
Baby's in the bathroom
Shooting boogers off the wall
(1999)

Down, Down Baby

Words
Down down baby

Down by the rollercoaster
Sweet, sweet, baby
I'll never let you go

Shimmy, shimmy, cocoa pop
Shimmy, shimmy, pop
Shimmy, shimmy, cocoa pop
Shimmy, shimmy, pow

Grandma, Grandma
Sick in bed
Called the doctor
And the doctor said
Let's get the rhythm of the head
Ding dong
Let's get the rhythm of the hands
Clap clap
Let's get the rhythm of the feet
Stomp stomp
Put it all together and
What do you get?
Ding dong, clap clap, stomp stomp

Say it all backwards and
What do you get?
Stomp stomp, clap clap [pause, pause]
Ding dong
(1992)[9]

Basic Motion
face partner and clap right palm up, left palm down, three times, pat partner's hands on 4
hands imitate a rollercoaster
hands imitate rocking a baby
hug self

clap like beginning three times; mock punch on "pow"

repeat first clapping moves
[imitative actions]

Alternate Ending

I had a <u>boyfriend</u>, cha <u>rumba</u>
<u>He</u> is a <u>cutie</u>, cha <u>rumba</u>
<u>Ice</u> cream, <u>milk</u> shake, <u>cherry</u> on <u>top</u>
<u>Ooh</u>, shawalawa
<u>Ooh</u>, shawalawa
<u>Ooh</u>, shawalawa
<u>Ooh</u>, sha<u>bang</u>bang
<u>Ooh</u>!
(1999)

Alternate Beginning

<u>Down</u> down <u>baby</u>, I can <u>shake</u> my <u>body</u>
<u>Down</u> down <u>baby</u>, I can <u>shake</u> my <u>body</u>
<u>Down</u> down <u>baby</u>, I can <u>do</u> <u>karate</u>
<u>Down</u> down <u>baby</u>, I can <u>call</u> my <u>mommy</u>
<u>Down</u> down <u>baby</u>, I can <u>call</u> my <u>brother</u>
<u>Down</u> down <u>baby</u>, I can <u>call</u> my <u>daddy</u>
(1999)

"Down Down Baby" is based on the 1969 pop song by Little Anthony and the Imperials that was reworked by rap artist Nelly in his 2000 hit "Country Grammar."

Chitty Chitty Bang Bang

Words	Basic Motion
<u>Chitty</u> chitty <u>bang</u> bang	pat hands around the circle
<u>Sitting</u> on a <u>fence</u>	repeat
<u>Trying</u> to make a <u>dollar</u>	
Out of <u>fifteen</u> <u>cents</u>	
She <u>missed</u>	cross legs and switch
She <u>missed</u>	cross legs and switch
She <u>missed</u> like <u>this</u>	cross legs and switch three times
(1999)[10]	

Down by the Banks

Words	Basic Motion
Down by the banks	pat neighbor's hands on beat
Of the hanky pank	she claps her neighbor's hands
Where the bullfrog jumped	she claps her neighbor's hands around the circle
From bank to bank	
Said ee-i-oh	
From the east to the west	
Where the curtains blow	[person patted on "blow" is out]
(1992, 1999)"	

Alternate Ending

> *From the east to the west*
> *Where the Kurtis Blow*
> *(1992)*

Kurtis Blow is a famous rapper and DJ from the early days of hip-hop.

Alternate Ending

> *Said ee-i-oh*
> *Your mother stinks and so do you*
> *Ping pong, Donkey Kong*
> *1, 2, 3, 4, 5, 6, 7, 8, 9, 10*
> *(1999)*

Mailman, Mailman

Words	Basic Motion
Mailman mailman	stand in circle
Do your duty	
'Cause here come miss American beauty	
She can do the pom pom	[imitative]
She can do the twist	
Most of all, she can make the boys kiss	
K-I-S-S	spread legs wider and wider until players fall over
(1999)	

Firecracker, Firecracker

Words	Basic Motion
Firecracker firecracker	clap, clap neighbor twice
Boom boom boom	clap neighbor along the circle, three times
Firecracker firecracker	
Boom boom boom	
The boys got the muscles	[imitative]
The teacher's got the brains	
The girls got the sexy legs and	
We won the game	
No! The girls got the muscles	
The girls got the brains	
And the girls got the sexy legs and	
We won the game	
(1999)	

The last stanza was improvised and led to much discussion about whether or not teachers had brains and whether boys were entitled to anything here. It always erupted in laughter.

Punchinella, Punchinella

Look who's here
Punchinella, Punchinella
Look who's here
Punchinella, in a shoe

What can you do
Punchinella, Punchinella
What can you do
Punchinella, in a shoe?

Oh, we can do it too
Punchinella, Punchinella
Oh, we can do it too
Punchinella, in a shoe

Oh, who do you choose

Punchinella, Punchinella
Oh, who do you choose
Punchinella, in a shoe?

(One girl sang, "Oh, We can look like idiots, Punchinella in a shoe.")

(1992)

Players circle the Punchinella, who does a motion, and everyone "does it too." The American version of this very old number imported from England was syncopated. It was the largest singing game ever performed at the Mill School, with dozens participating, but it was performed only once, on Mardi Gras.[12]

STEPS

In 1991, I saw four African American girls doing what looked like a dance step. "Is that a step?" I asked. I was wondering whether the dance was choreographed or they were improvising. "*No*, no, *this* is a *step*." Step, *clap*, rock, *clap*, step, *clap*, rock *clap*. They rocked gently back and forth, clapping their hands lightly on the off beat. At first they sang quietly, but it built into a roar.

Pump It Up

Words	Basic Motion
Pump, pump, pump, pump pump it up	tap palms around the circle to start
Pump, pump, pump it up	step clap, rock clap [2x]
Well, my name is [player's name]	step clap, rock clap
Pump it up	step clap, rock clap
That's what they call me	[repeat]
Pump it up	
My sign is [astrological sign]	
Pump it up	
And I can work that body, oddy, oddy	shake and improvise
Make sure, you don't hurt that body	
Pump, pump, pump, pump	
Pump it up	
(1992)	

The phrase *pump it up* appears in several recordings, including "Pump up the Jam" by M. Kamosi and T. De Quincy from 1989. Each girl gets a chance to say her name and her astrological sign and work her body.

Pump It Up

Traditional
Transcribed by Anna Beresin
and Larry Cohen

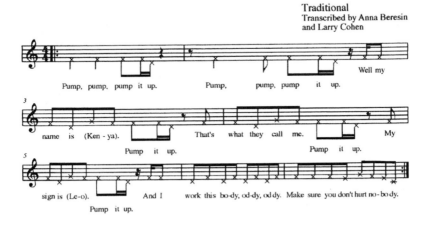

Stepping is the African American art of polyrhythmic hand clapping and foot stomping that is a circle or line game, often with call-and-response singing and turn taking. A proud tradition at many predominantly African American schools and among African American groups at predominantly white institutions, steps are akin to cheerleading and a cousin to both hand clapping and marching.[13] The steps performed in the Mill School yard exclusively concerned the body, skill, and the complex role of being an attractive young woman. They involved singing, clapping, stamping feet, and improvising with other steppers. Although professional or competitive steppers are both male and female, only girls engaged in stepping on the playground. The rhythms are complex and syncopated, and the formation is typically a small circle. In most cases, each stepper is introduced by name and given a chance to perform a solo move.

Unlike rope rhymes, step lyrics tend to be overtly sexual. Steps were taken much more seriously than hand-clapping games, which usually ended in laughter.[14] Some traditional step themes involve ritual insults: poverty, physical ugliness, stupidity, and promiscuity.[15] Rarely recorded among females, especially young females, ritual insults are a way of practicing coolheadedness about the body in an insulting world.[16] Originally expurgated from collections of children's lore, taboo rhymes such as these have been recorded for what they are: honest reflections of the issues with which real children wrestle.

The girls who did double-dutch jump rope also did steps, which were exclusively the domain of African American working-class girls at the Mill School, those who traveled by bus from less affluent neighborhoods. It was a secret repertoire of the body, sometimes labeled "nasty" by the girls themselves. But when they were assured they would not get in trouble for singing to me, they sang louder than they did for "Big Mac" or any rope rhyme. Stepping offered the girls a chance to improvise and "show your motions."

Because the Mill School children considered steps special and rare, and because none of these steps has previously been recorded, I offer their transcription into approximate musical notation. The jump rope rhymes have the tap of the rope to guide us, and the rock and roll numbers have been recorded in one version or another.

Shoo, Shoo Sharida

Words	Basic Motion
Shoo, _shoo_ Sharida	step, step clap, rock clap
My _name_ is _Violet_	step, step clap, rock clap
Shoo _shoo_ Sharida	
That's _what_ they _call_ me	
Shoo, _shoo_ Sharida	
My _sign_ is _Pisces_	
Shoo, _shoo_ Sharida	
And I can _break_ it down	improvise

Shoo, _shoo_ Sharida
Real _sexy_ now
Shoo, _shoo_ Sharida
Now _take_ my _goal_ post
_(1992)_

Shoo, Shoo Sharida

Traditional
Transcribed by Anna Beresin
and Larry Cohen

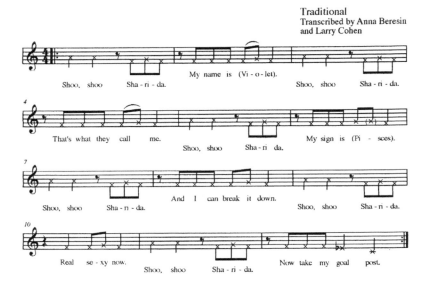

Fly Girl

Words

Fly girl, fly girl
Go girl, go girl

My <u>name</u> is Coco, <u>I'm</u> a <u>supa</u>fly <u>girl</u>
I <u>float</u> like a <u>butterfly</u>
<u>Sting</u> like a <u>bee</u>
<u>That's</u> why they <u>call</u> me

<u>Fly</u> girl
<u>Go</u> Coco, Go <u>Coco</u>
(1999)

Basic Motion

scissor feet, clap
scissor feet, clap

improvise

Fly Girl

Traditional
Transcribed by Anna Beresin
and Larry Cohen

Fly girl, Fly girl.   Go girl, Go girl.   My name is (Cocoa), I'm a su-per fly girl,   I

float like a but - ter - fly,   sting like a bee.   That's   why they call   me ---

Hollywood

Word	Basic Motion
Hollywood got *Meeca*	in pairs, in two lines, retreating
Hollywood got *Meeca*	right rocks back, left in place
Hollywood got *Meeca*	right in place, pause, clap
And *always do*	repeat until the end

[Meeca]
Well, it looks like me got number 20
Watch the power of the money
If you see me on the street
Hey girl, you better speak

[all]
Hey, you think you bad
[Meeca]
Me? I know I'm bad

[all]
Hey, you think you cute
[Meeca]
Cute, fine, sexy, too

[all]
Hey, you think you fine
[Meeca]
I'm fine, I'll blow your mind

I got a man, he's twenty-nine
Tic tac Paddy whack
Who you think you looking at?
A-B-C-D Gonna have a baby

Reese's pieces butter cup
If you next I wish you luck

[all]
Hollywood got Licia
Hollywood got Licia
Hollywood got Licia
And always do

[Licia]
Well, it looks like me got number 4
Watch the prowler at the door
If you see me on the street
Hey you better speak to me

[all]
Hey, you think you bad
[Licia]
Least I pick my maxi pad

[all]
Hey, you think you cute
[Licia]
Least I'm not a prostitute

[all]
Hey, you think you fine
[Licia]
I'm fine, I'll blow your mind

I got a man, he's twenty-nine
Tic tac Paddy whack
Who you think you looking at?
A-B-C-D Gonna have a baby

Reese's pieces butter cup
If you next I wish you luck
(1992)

Hollywood
Chorus

Traditional
Transcribed by Anna Beresin
and Larry Cohen

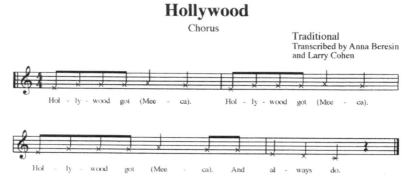

Hol - ly - wood got (Mee - ca).   Hol - ly - wood got (Mee - ca).

Hol - ly - wood got (Mee - ca).   And al - ways do.

See the text for the traditional rap.

Telephone

Words

Telephone, tel, telephone
Telephone, tel, telephone
Yo Tasha
Yo
You're wanted on the telephone
Who is it?
A boy
I know what he wants
He wants my lips, my tits

Basic Motion

basic step, clap, step, clap as above, only slower

repeat

pointing shyly

My grass and my ass

Telephone, tel, telephone
Telephone, tel, telephone
Yo Tasha
Yo

You're wanted on the telephone
Who is it?

Your man
I know what he wants
He wants my lips, my tits

My grass and my ass
Telephone, tel, telephone
Telephone, tel, telephone
Yo Tasha
Yo

You're wanted on the telephone
Who is it?

A girl
I know what she wants
She wants my man
Goddamn
She's getting out of hand

Telephone, tel, telephone
Telephone, tel, telephone
Yo Tasha
Yo

You're wanted on the telephone
Who is it?

Your ex
I know what he wants
He wants my lips, my tits
My grass and my ass
(1992)

Telephone

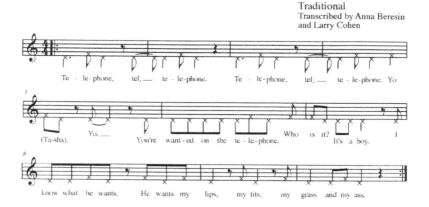

Traditional
Transcribed by Anna Beresin
and Larry Cohen

I Work

Words

I <u>wo-rk</u>, <u>all</u> year
I <u>wo-rk</u>, <u>all</u> year
I <u>wo-rk</u>, <u>all</u> year
I <u>work</u> I <u>work</u> I <u>work</u>

Now <u>watch</u> Coco <u>work</u> her <u>hips</u>

Basic Motion

scissor legs and land on beat
slow hip sway left to right on "work"

scissor legs quickly three times

She <u>wo-rks</u>, <u>all</u> year
She <u>wo-rks</u>, <u>all</u> year
She <u>wo-rks</u>, <u>all</u> year
She <u>works</u>, she <u>works</u>, she <u>works</u>

Now <u>watch</u> all of us <u>work</u>
We <u>wo-rk</u>, <u>all</u> year
We <u>wo-rk</u>, <u>all</u> year
We <u>wo-rk</u>, <u>all</u> year
We <u>work</u>, we <u>work</u>, we <u>work</u>
(1992)

I Work

Traditional
Transcribed by Anna Beresin
and Larry Cohen

Whether they were playing with taboo words or roles, practicing cooperation, practicing rhythm or dance moves, or exploring new ways of moving their young bodies, these girls had the pleasure of choice. The songs seemed to emerge randomly, but in reality, someone had the idea or the memory of a bit of a song, and group members worked together to re-create the songs on the spot.

Traditional games and traditional "old school" rhymes were clearly about the body—as it grows, as it experiments, as it negotiates with other bodies. The body is the subject and the object of traditional play across genres. Mixing the genres together resulted in competitive songs (cooperatively played), cooperative songs (competitively danced), seriously silly songs, and silly songs that were about very serious matters. In their entirety, these songs possess a dreaminess as well as an urgent sense of personal power. As a group, they form a treasure trove of ingredients on which the children can draw when and where they need these materials. "We learn songs. . . like, our mothers. . . they learned from their mothers. We learned from them."

This larger view offers a reminder that no one type or genre is loudest in the school yard, yet some messages still remain privileged. Games change; old themes are updated and new themes are added. It is a dreamy but uneven playing field.

- 7 -

KEYWORDS OF THE PLAYGROUND

My initial study of the Mill School was never intended to be longitudinal, but I kept going back. After starting out as a study of ethnic diversity, my project shifted to focus on culture change. Like most folklorists, I sought to examine the uniqueness of the location and the variants that could be recorded—the songs, the stories, the moves. I was curious about how the children negotiated spatially across the concrete grid in the shadow of schooling. I remained interested in viewing play as a kind of communicative negotiation, an alternative and much more amusing window into childhood than was typically studied.

I would stop by the Mill School, located a few minutes from my home, and find myself using the original data as a baseline. The graffiti would be painted over and return, little ones became the experts, games remained the same even as teachers moved on to other jobs. Game locations floated slightly from one wall to another, like shifting shorelines. My field notes and audiovisual material piled higher and higher, and I realized that the cumulative knowledge, this quantifiable pile, could turn snapshots of games into useful social science.

I became convinced that children's folklore was sociologically and psychologically significant, not just a charming souvenir. This idea is very difficult to prove, in part because of the semiconscious nature of children's play. Traditional ethnographic interviews did not offer the desired insight, since the children were often in a dreamlike state of play, or became giddy with the audiovisual playback, or were too focused on not getting in trouble.

Violent behavior was easily coded. The texts of singing games and the popularity of ball games were easily counted. Variations could easily be recorded, as in the tradition of most collectors of children's folklore. But dramatic gestures and words were all over the school yard, not just in singing games and mock aggression, not just reflections of children's cultures as a subset of adult cultures. I realized that I needed to demonstrate the playground's keywords and key gestures, the hollered and the silent, which grown-ups may overlook. These shouts and repeated motions are another form of ethnographic evidence, an extreme vocabulary of children's culture outside the genre-specific coding of games and conflict.

Social theorist Raymond Williams has utilized the concept of keywords to demonstrate the vocabulary and literal contents of a particular milieu.[1] Rooted in the practice of "corpus linguistics" (the counting of samples in real-world texts), the practice has been challenged by Noam Chomsky's cognitive linguistic approach, which acknowledges that language is created in context, performed among players. The playground allows us to examine verbal and nonverbal phrases that repeat and demand our attention.

Although Williams attempted to define and show the historical roots of keywords ranging from art to folk to violence, newer attempts to revise his groundbreaking work have struggled, as words have meaning in context and float like generalized half-truths when removed. For grown-ups, all of us expatriates from children's culture, a translation of some essential keywords of the playground follows. But it does not reflect every playground or every childhood, nor is it in any way complete. These are the terms and the battles of the yard at the Mill School, a working-class, multiracial public elementary at the turn of the millennium. Readers may see similarities to playgrounds they know, but all words and struggles are not necessarily the same.

THE CHILDREN'S PLAYGROUND KEYWORDS

I intentionally focus here on the vocabulary that is unique to the children's cultures, not the vocabulary of children's struggles with the adult cultures of commercialism and with the school's institutionalized power, which are addressed in previous chapters. Children's peer culture and its stylizations, or children's folklore, are a subset of these struggles but are not merely so. An island may belong to an archipelago, but it has its own characteristics.

Each game has its own language. Jump rope, Sui, ball, steps, and numbers have individual histories, rules, aesthetics, and vocabulary. All are associated with overlapping subcultures within children's culture, yet a vocabulary of the playground transcends that of the game. These are the words of the body, of challenge, of aesthetics, and of socialization.

Roger Abrahams has recently addressed key terms in contemporary folklore study.[2] Although they have guided my training, the terms *performance, vernacular, identity, community, text,* and *genre* are useful in thinking about the stylizations of folklife but not of the playground per se. Like Abrahams, I seek a host of terms that come from the people I study as well as the terms that can appear only from a distance, a distinction linguist Kenneth Pike has called the emic and the etic.[3] The native perspective is essential, as anthropology has taught us, but seeing patterns requires views from a variety of angles, near and far.

The etic, or outside, view can be obscured by a specific agenda. In the early days of the collection of children's folklore, mid-twentieth-century practitioners worked under the influence of nationalism. Like folktales, folk songs, and folk dances, games were hailed as reflections of national character, showing the uniqueness of a specific culture.[4] Next followed an equally distorted view of games as examples of panhuman poetry, with the assumption that the performances of the texts were less of an issue than their seemingly similar formats.[5] In contrast to these frailties of folklore and early cultural studies, psychology's weakness was that it missed the forest for the trees. Studies of individuals were somehow seen as representing groups, and studies of groups typically took a viewpoint so removed that individuals and their cultural stylizations became altogether invisible.

The true intellectual predecessors of this study are the sociological classics of street-corner ethnography, studies that included local men's voices and placed them in the larger social and cultural struggle of that time and location.[6] I hope that childhood study will emerge in the same way, as a collection of valuable smaller studies that can then be seen as a set of truths, worthy of examination.

The games and other activities of the playground are linked through this sense of common vocabulary—childhood's common vocabulary on this one street-corner playground. Guided by the principle, first introduced in chapter 2, of qualitative and quantitative markers, these terms reflect passion and frequency. They emerge from the children's emotional, qualitative investment and were repeated in many genres on many occasions, giving the terms quantitative power. They are the children's terms.

Play

Play is "what we kids do," the activity of playing. It can be seen, heard, recorded, and played back, but it is also in the head. It is how children spend their time.[7] Play is considered "fun," a circular argument that is not nearly as sophisticated as the phrase "what we kids do." I asked, "If a person from Mars came down and said 'What is this weird thing you do at 10:30?' what would you say?" "Play!" they chorused. "We go and play."

Skill

According to the children, *skill* is "what you're good at," a socially recognizable talent, specific to a specific kind of play. The idea resembles but is not the same as "what you know," a coded way of saying "your tradition." Skill is related to the notion of challenge, which itself depends on skill/tradition. Each game requires a particular set of skills, and each player in each genre spoke of who "got skills."

Challenge

Challenge makes a specific game or activity harder. It exists in the game and can be added at any time as a form of competition. It is visible in rope games and handball games, hopscotch, ball, and tag and is the essence of folk variation. "Challenge!" is often heard around the yard. "Challenge!" A player must throw the handball from where it has been caught. "Challenge!" A jumper must repeat the double-dutch rope pattern exactly as the previous jumper has performed it. "Challenge, Challenge, 1, 2, 3." The children challenge themselves, their minds, their bodies, and each other. The grown-ups find the whole school yard a challenge.

Jump

Sometimes used as a way of indicating which player's turn it is, *jump* refers to the physical act of having to move to play. "Gotta get my jump." Sometimes used as a substitute for *move* or *movement*. Jumps appeared in basketball, rope, hopscotch, and in the informal body play of mock violence. Given the medically established connection between weight-bearing exercise and bone building, are children stimulating their physical growth by jumping? The urgent theme of the moving, growing, body lies at the core of almost every singing game. *Jump* also has power associations: if someone is "jumped," he or she has been attacked. Jumping, getting one's turn, is related to survival.

Freebie

A freebie is a gift, an offer of a jump, without calling it. It is offered as a sign of friendship, of status, of nonnegotiated participation. A token of free play, freebies are both nothing and cherished.

Calling It

Most activities had to be "called" ahead of time, setting up order, establishing rules, and marking out turf at the end of a period for the next play period. Students "called it" in hopscotch, in rope, in handball; they even called who had the court in basketball. Similar to the pregame ceremonies of counting out, calling is a quick way of establishing peer-created order before players have even gathered. "Spit, spit, you are not it" could be heard quietly, reverently, with the lead child pointing to himself or herself and counting around a circle, until the last one remaining had been chosen as it.[8] Calling could be used to choose captains; choose order; allow certain types of movements, such as bendsies and helpsies; and even reverse previously made arrangements. "Ace Ace No Higher." " No reverse it down." Calling it makes the game fair.

Doing/Going

The children perceived the school yard as being about how they "did" things. "This is how you do ball." "Watch us do rope." For children, play is doing. Doing reflects the centrality of the body, which is celebrated and/or cautioned against in almost every traditional song. Going gets them to do the doing. They "go" and do a game. They go play. Even games that are traditional were said to be made up, pointing to the active, creative process of gaming.

Danger/Safety
In/Out
Fair/Foul
It/Not It
Ours/Theirs

These opposites cover the challenges of specific games. The ultimate reflections of social power, these markings help define boundaries in the surreal mix of play. These opposites turn the logic of game play into both the personal realm and a territorial framework, a way of indicating turf and boundaries of social identity. Used as a mask for social inclusion, these terms creatively link the game world to social subcultures.

All of these terms are embodied dynamisms, reflecting how the school yard is a site for processing the many struggles of childhood itself. No matter the topic—personal, interpersonal, cultural, historical—the playground serves as the children's emotional battleground, where they are fought over by the institution of school, corporations, and misguided adults who conceive of childhood in rigid ways.

LAUGHTER AND SCREAMING

Sound is as native to the playground as movement is. At every presentation of my audio- or videotapes, adults have braced themselves after hearing the flood of sound that erupts. "No relay . . . you got ends . . . Big Mac Filet o' Fish . . . Work that body, oddy, oddy." Screaming emerges out of the excitement of play, out of frustration, and out of social distance, often initiating or transitioning a game with nonsense. Laughter punctuates most games and is made up of the motions of the mouth, the head, the shoulders, the stomach, and the arms. Laughter ranges from the smallest giggle to the uproarious guffaw.[9] All of these sounds have ripple effects, creating more sound and more motion. A silent playground is one without play as we know it.

CULTURAL PHRASES

In addition to the ethnic stylization of terms relevant to traditional game forms, cultural layers appear in each genre: words of commercials (Nike, Big Mac, Reebok), or American culture (red, white, bluesies), local culture (North Philly, the Philadelphia Eagles) or pop culture (MC Hammer and Pac Man). These phrases echo the dreamy cultural layers in their storytelling (Reebok Walkers, "Don't go to California or you'll get shot," "There's been an accident on the boulevard," *Pet Sematary*). As playwright Augusto Boal suggests, "Games are a dialogue."[10]

Dialogues among players, between genres, and within the brain of the moving child create *gamestories*. Keep-away and tag ooze in and around basketball and hopscotch. The basketball rolls through the jump rope. Hand claps or steps occupy rope jumpers awaiting their turns. The pregame ceremonies of counting out or choosing sides are as much stories, enactments of power struggles large and small, as any formal narrative or organized game. In a sense, the term *gamestories* is my synonym for what play looks like. The content changes from moment to moment and place to place.

CHANGING KEYWORDS

Girls' Games/Boys' Games

The children recognized that some games were closed but also acknowledged that these boundaries had changed over time. In the early 1990s, girls did not play Sui (but some boys played at home with their sisters); ten years later, girls played Sui in the school yard every day. Boys in general do not jump rope, but several girls knew of boys who jumped competitively in jump rope leagues. Football in general was played by boys, but Susie played "'cause she can catch." The children acknowledged the existence of gendered patterns but considered them contemporary practices rather than facets embedded in the games themselves.

By 2004, girls as well as boys skillfully tossed footballs, and female basketball players completed for space at the single hoop remaining in the Mill School yard. Girls' folk games reflected the changes in the larger cultural landscape—the rise of females in professional sports and the workplace. Gender division has not disappeared—nor should it—but has become more flexible and fluid than earlier writings have suggested.[11]

BLACK CHILDREN'S GAMES AND WHITE CHILDREN'S GAMES

None of the students verbally acknowledged that some games were played solely by either white or black children. Yet children who crossed over into new games—white girls who turned for double-dutch or middle-class African American girls who halfheartedly but interestedly imitated steps—reflected the hidden vocabulary of race in this multiracial place. Race was neither overtly addressed nor a source of direct tension, but the children acknowledged a certain social bravery—bravery was their word—among those who stepped into games from other traditions.

In 1991, girls' games were rarely racially integrated, although boys games mixed easily. By 1999, hopscotch and double-dutch were racially integrated, with multiple ropes of both white and black children playing together and in parallel. By 2004, much of the desegregation on the playground was gone, in part reflecting the decreased integration of the school itself. With the demise of the desegregation program, both the inside of the school and its yard returned to what Jonathan Kozol calls "apartheid schooling."[12]

VIOLENCE

Grown-ups mentioned violence and used it as an excuse to limit play. But as discussed earlier, the illusion of violence was created by the stressful transition between play and class time, when teachers would retrieve their students and see violence. This keyword needs to be changed.

Other phrases are also not found in the school yard.

"Recess Is Like Afterschool Play"

I received a variety of responses when I asked children what they did after school.

I like to get on the bus and do my homework. That's a break. Yes, it is.

I eat. Sleep.

I take my dog out. I play free throw with [another child]. Sometimes my dad takes me to these gyms and everything. They have exercises, swimming pool, ping-pong.

After school on Tuesdays I go to ceramics. Then I call my friends, play with my sister.

(Do you play Sui at home?)

No.

I play basketball.

I play wall ball.

And football.

I go home and ride my bike, play with my dog.

I do my homework and then play outside.

I like to go home and not do my homework.

Go outside and play run the bases with my friends. We live on the same street.

Play wall ball.

First, I do safety [patrol], then I go home, do my homework, and watch TV. Wait, sometimes I go to Gina's baseball games and her gymnastics practice, and sometimes Gina goes over to my house. And on Fridays I go down to my grandmother's house, and I play down there.

Sometimes I get my mother to take me to the mall, and I shop with my allowance money. And at night I do my homework.

Sometimes after school I watch <u>Rags to Riches</u>.

Most of these activities bore little similarity to the games played at recess. Children are busy with homework and other tasks; when they play, they do so mostly alone or with one other person. A few children who lived on streets with others and had parental permission had some kind of group experience, but that situation was the exception rather than the rule.

"Too Old to Play"

What of the notion, first expressed by the Mill School's principal, that children aged ten and above were told old to play? Does recess differ for kids of different ages? I asked the fourth-graders, who were next in line to lose their playtime, for their opinions.

Yeah, there is a difference.

First to sixth.

Because the older kids act [like] they're all cool.

And the little kids act they're playing ponies or He Man [giggles].

Or Cinderella.

Seventh or eighth don't have recess. They only have lunch and they have a little thing after that.

(Is that better or worse?)

Worse.

It's better for them, 'cause they don't think, you know, recess is—

They need to learn, so they can go to college.

(So they don't play any more once they get to seventh grade?)

That's the way that my sister is going.

I will!

(You will?)

They don't have any recess. All they do is go outside.

They have a little recess after lunch.

(At what age do you think—you say the kids stop playing, start talking? When does that happen to you at recess?)

Some people sit at their line, where their line is, and talk.

(Does that happen at a certain age? Like all of a sudden when you hit sixth grade you stop playing?)

No.

No, some people—

They still play.

My sister's in seventh grade, and she still plays Barbies with me.

My sister's in ninth grade, and she still plays Barbies with me.

My sister plays everything with me.

Michelle, Michelle's in high school—that's ninth grade—and she plays house.

(Well, there you go.)

She babysits me.

'Cause she plays house with me.

Although older children still play, they add talk to the traditional play styles of childhood—that is, they enlarge their vocabulary rather than stop playing. Intergenerational activities offer an opportunity for play and allow older children the opportunity to be multilingual, to play/speak gamestories in the manner of different ages.

There is an elder day care center across the street from the Mill School. What now seems like radical lawbreaking and symbolic violence pales in comparison to what took place three-quarters of a century ago. In the first half of the twentieth century, pranks—including some involving significant danger from cars—were common. "We'd tie strings to one another's doors across the avenue so that when one opened, the other slammed shut." "We'd play chicken with the trucks, daring each other to cross." "There was a lot of stuff we did that involved cow turds." Moreover, the senior citizens play bingo every week—they understand children's need to play. Some of those with whom I spoke told me that they live for bingo. A game of chance, it is perceived as a game of skill, of survival, of beating the odds of decline and loss. "It keeps your brains moving," one octogenarian told me, mirroring the earnestness of the ten-year-olds across the street in the Mill School yard.

The denizens of the elder care center begin their bingo games with dull eyes, softly calling out "Bingo" when they win. By the second round, the winner gets more excited; color returns to the players' faces. By the third round, eyes flash and adrenalin surges; people begin to bounce a little in their seats. Soon, "Bingo" is shouted clearly and loudly, and the players smile and move in their chairs. When the lights dim at the end of the game, the elders return to their bodies. The center's activities director muses that no one is too old to play: "It's hope they're after."

- 8 -

PLAY AND PARADOX

Theorists have been fighting over what play is and is not as educators dispute what is or is not a worthwhile activity for children. For years, writers have argued that we do not know quite what play is, but we all recognize it when we see it.[1] Sadly, this is not the case.

But documentation—film, audio, painting, and even recollection—can help grown-ups remember what play is about. Although strong disagreement exists about what play does biologically, socially, and emotionally for children, its characteristics are indeed recognizable:

- it is associated with quick, darting movements;[2]
- it is doubly messaged, an it and a not it, safe but not quite so, a light-hearted yet serious attitude;[3]
- it is typically a miniature or exaggerated version of the larger reality, whether imitating battle, hunting, courtship, or work;[4]
- it is impossible to see without its frame—that is, the fight in the fighting ring, the ball game with its boundaries, the rope game within its rope, the hand-clapping game within its circle of friends;[5]
- it is fundamentally social, even if one is playing solely with one's alternative self, one's imagined partner;
- it is associated with change, even though games are associated with rules and consistency. One plays a game, in a sense, to break the rules

- Games that have no play are no fun, robotic, repetitive, unimaginative, and sometimes a lot like gym.

Above all, play is what children do. It is what they are passionate about, what they think about, talk about, perfect in their spare time. At its best, it makes them happy. In its struggle, it makes them work hard at skill building. The job of adults is to provide children with the opportunity to do what they need to do, the time to do it, and the assurance that they can do it without harming each other.

If school is a place for learning what the culture values, then play, with its subtext of cultural change, can be seen as inherently threatening that culture—but only if one has a static vision of education or human growth. Typically, play is least respected in places that have a narrow range of acceptable behaviors, whether it is an elite school with unrealistic expectations of performance or a working-class school with unrealistic expectations of teacher power. But teachers lack the ability to override culture, much as they might wish they had such power. Forcing children to abandon play turns them into contortionists or, worse, leads them to be silent and drains the fire from their eyes.

Researchers, theorists, and educators must maintain respect for paradox and avoid letting the strangeness of research turn into tragic irony. In this case, that idea would translate into the removal of the opportunity for play. Play confuses, some argue, so let us be rid of it—sit the children down, medicate them, prevent them from speaking. Instead, it is much better to see what children are trying to tell us as they yell, jump, and clap. Their offerings are childhood's gifts; in return, they deserve our protection.

David Swartz fine-tunes Pierre Bourdieu's view of fieldwork: "Field analysis, therefore, directs the researcher's attention to a level of analysis of revealing the integrating logic of competition between opposing viewpoints."[6] Teacher and child, corporation and school, game circle to game circle—the playground asks us to see concentric, overlapping, and conflicting circles. In essence, it requires us to see the world as sociologists from conflicting schools of sociology—as structural-functionalists and as conflict theorists. There are wholes and tensions, and both are real. With each game played and its corresponding cultural shift, the study of childhood emerges as a study of motion rather than a temporarily fixed or constant state or stage.[7] The paradox of the research lies in its shifting truths: what was once true is no longer necessarily true; some things were never true.

In illustrating the multiplicity of truths and their changes over time, I have linked various theorists in larger conceptual pairs and trios. Seeing the playground as the children do requires negotiating these theorists' ideas, even if the writers themselves do not know each other. Paradoxes acknowledge that opposite truths can simultaneously exist; complexity reveals depth, not necessarily conflict. We can call these the observable paradoxes of the playground:

- Trivial, small things may be hugely significant
  (psychological paradoxes: Benjamin's Paradox of Toys, Erikson's Paradox of Play, and Piaget's Paradox of Games);
- Children's culture simultaneously creates and conserves its own culture and adult culture over time
  (folkloric and sociological paradoxes: Newell's Paradox and Willis's Paradox);
- Play, in its ambiguity, can be studied by studying its frame, which itself can be played with
  (sociocultural paradoxes: Bateson's Fighting Paradox, Goffman's Situation Paradox, and Sutton-Smith's Play Paradox);
- Violence may be the symptom and/or the cause of social problems
  (sociological and critical theory paradoxes: Foucault and Bourdieu's Violence Paradox).

Children have their own way of holding onto meaning through multiple dialectics in a given whole—through games, arguing about fair and foul, out and safe, in and out. Children are frame-specific and spend most of their time testing such concepts with their words and their bodies. They live in a world of strangeness and paradox and are compelled to make sense of things the best they can. These prepubescent philosophers of play have given us more to think about:

- Tashi's Paradox: Quantity can be a significant indicator of culture, and passion can be a significant indicator of culture ("Nike" and "Big Fat Stick");

- Tyron's Paradox: An infinite number of cultural and emotional references and struggles are copresent in the playground even though they are not always audible or visible (Freddy and *Pet Sematary*);
- Marcus's Paradox: Games, like stories, are a form of commentary that the players, tellers, or singers may or may not be aware that they are expressing ("The Newses" and "I Work");
- Kirsten's Paradox: Things change because they no longer serve a purpose or because they serve an important purpose ("Cinderella" and "The Queen Is a Snake");
- Mikee's Paradox: Gendered activity or ethnic activity is a reflection of a historically specific framework, and categories are both real and illusions (Suicide Handball, rope);
- Jenny's Paradox: Well-intentioned activity can lead to passivity, and emptiness can lead to activity (hopscotch and the Fighting Game).

To this list I add one more idea:

- Children can create happiness for themselves even in unfavorable situations, but that does not mean that unfavorable situations are helpful.

The battles of the Mill School playground are themselves paradoxical: this playground is violent only in transition, but the place is filled with symbolic violence. The battles are there: in bodily urgency, power over scripted speech, the tug-of-war over turf and friendship, the fight over the right to have a playtime at all. But paradoxes, the opposite truisms of the strange beauty of life itself, are worth playing with.[8]

Two ironies emerge from the literature of the playground:

- Recess, when it is not trivialized, is hailed for what it can do for classroom's benefit—that is, better concentration, more focused work—rather than for the benefits of play.[9]
- Play is hailed for its individual expressive or medical contributions rather than its complex cultural and social offerings, even though recess brings together hundreds of children to play.[10]

These two ironies reflect the core findings of recent recess publications: recess benefits both individual learning and individual health.

Both are important contributions, but hidden are the social benefits, the cultural digestion, the expressivity of games. Peter Blatchford's longitudinal study is the most socially conscious of these works, stating that recess is "an important and productive context (at all ages) for developing skills in friendship relations and social networks, and conflict management."[11] Anthony Pellegrini, perhaps the most prolific recess researcher, goes as far as to say that "many of the behaviors that children exhibit on the playground are powerful predictors of competence."[12] Yet again, these authors emphasize the individual's competence, the individual's skill set.

The biggest boost to recess has been the publication of a recent study led by Romina Barros that followed eleven thousand third-graders and found that those with at least fifteen minutes of recess were "better behaved" in the classroom. Most important, Barros and her coauthors suggest that the removal of recess harms children and note that the 30 percent of the children studied who had no or minimal breaks were more likely to be black, to come from lower-income homes, and to live in urban settings.[13] These findings were reported in the *New York Times*[14] and led to a flurry of Internet activity by parents frustrated by their children's lack of recess despite its obvious utility.

Science tends to reduce fields into answerable questions. But the danger is visible in the dryness that overtakes the vast majority of research about children. I believe oppression needs research, a distillation of the problems so that they can be addressed. But stories and art require more stories and art. Recess is clearly needed, but it is not simply reducible to physical education class, to sweat, or to brain-boosting rest. Even the *New York Times Magazine*'s celebrated feature, "Taking Play Seriously,"[15] shows only children moving individually, no two together. Image after image of the lone jumping child. It is as if we have a hard time accepting the cultural value of group, expressive motion. It is as if we need to rationalize the arts.

The push and pull of cultural forces sometimes makes it appear that children's play is in danger of disappearing. Folklorist June Factor refers to this phenomenon as one of the myths of children's folklore.[16] Opportunities for expression in schools are being constricted, but play remains very much alive. My research suggests that play is changing, and change is what play does best. African American girls teach immigrants and working-class white girls how to jump double-dutch. Eleven- and twelve-year-olds teach their younger peers how to play commercial games; in turn, the younger children edit culture to serve their needs. As the Mill School has moved toward greater gender equality, racial inequality moved first forward and then backward.

Working-class children of all ethnicities were more experimental, reflecting a physical mobility untapped by their middle-class peers. Throughout the duration of this study, the mobile children came from the working classes. This finding suggests that policies that restrict movement limit working-class children the most.

So much literature on gender neglects race, and so much literature on race neglects class. Scores of books generalize about children who fight, children who create, children with troubles, painting childhood with so broad a brushstroke that one feels compelled to shout, "But that's not true for Susie! Or Karim! Or Tommy!" The Mill School's middle-class black girls do not jump double-dutch or engage in stepping. Girls and children of color now have opportunities that did not previously exist, but they still do not have equal access. Boys are as passionate about their skills and their arts as are the girls.

Games—and by extension recess—serve as a testing ground, a lending library for trying on "otherness." Children utilize game genres to test boundaries while simultaneously conserving culture. The school yard is a laboratory of socialization, and children use the time to learn how to follow rules, how to rewrite them when necessary, and how to make mistakes and do so gracefully. The school yard rather than the school offers social mobility. The transition rather than the playtime is violent.

Paul Willis, a writer of youth, social class, and common culture, asks, "What exactly is produced by symbolic work and symbolic creativity?" He answers, "First and perhaps most important, they produce and reproduce individual identities—who and what 'I am' and could become. Second, symbolic work and creativity place identities in larger wholes. Third and finally, symbolic work and creativity develop and affirm our active senses of our own vital capacities, the power of the self and how they might be applied to the cultural world."[17]

Play emerges as nothing less than the serious negotiation of individual expression and culture.[18] In essence, the school yard is designated for the pull of significant disordering opposites, providing a place where the weak can feel powerful, the smart can act foolish, danger can be made safe, and both those labeled skilled and unskilled can shine with sweat. Through the games' ordering and disordering and the physical freedom of movement, the student body edits culture.

CONCLUSION
Wrestling with the School Yard

When the Mill School's teachers saw the videos of their school yard, several remarked that the children "were just being good for the camera." After I assured the teachers that the children were just as busy and kind-spirited when the camera was obscured from view, they became nostalgic about childhood and curious about what the children were singing—whether the songs were the same as the ones the teachers had sung in their youth. What was old, they asked, and what was new? Does recess matter?

Grown-ups are experiencing a crisis of misunderstanding regarding children's play. If it does not seem to make sense, it is labeled trivial and a waste of time. But each activity contains a series of layers—game content and form, style and participation—all in various states of stability and mobility. Most importantly and most consistently, recess offers moving activities in an environment that is edited, even in minute ways, by children themselves and is framed by the larger institutions of power.

Ironically, many adults find precisely this peer empowerment distasteful. Peer power might lead to disrespect and is consequently belittled. Touch might lead to injury and is therefore eliminated. Words might lead to insults, so lunches sometimes must be silent. Movement might lead to falling, so students must walk rather than run. Performance might lead to failure, so recorded music must be used for musical stage shows. Art might be too expressive, so stencil work created by grown-ups and carefully copied by children must adorn the school windows each season and the hopscotches each fall. Playground games are synonymous with risk—physical risk, emotional risk, intellectual risk, social risk, and cultural risk. Peer empowerment apparently is more distasteful than scripting by Nike and other big corporations and the punishments administered by big fat sticks, perhaps because children more easily controlled.

Why, then, do grown-ups have such difficulty seeing positive activity on the playground? "The eye and the brain see only that order in the world that they are ready to see," writes chaos scholar R. J. Bird.[1] Perhaps working-class children's play life is difficult to see because working-class adulthood is also difficult to see. "Work that body, oddy, oddy, make sure you don't hurt that body," "I work, I work, I work," "Hop to the N-I-K-E," "Who you think you looking at?" "There been an accident yesterday on the boulevard, truck turned over and truck blew up. That's it—no more newses today."

Because children describe games as the playground's main focal points, their gamestories merit a more central position in the study of childhood. Film, interviews, and paintings demonstrate the world of ball and the world of hopscotch. Children organize their playgrounds into understandable units. Jump rope predictably happens in one of two spots, and there is a definite range of thematic material. Wall ball is traditionally played on two specific walls. The lone tree (or a significant roving grown-up) serves as base. Subculture is really based on common activity, not just gender, race, ethnicity, class, or age, all of which are more fluid than we have supposed.

True chaotic systems show "order in disorder" in a closed system. The playground is anything but chaotic. It responds to the changes in the children's ecosystem, in economics, and in demographics and reacts to new roles through the art of play.

Folklorists and anthropologists note that culture is an extension of the order in our own minds, which is in turn framed by traditional ways of seeing.[2] Upon reflection, our ways of dealing with children as a disempowered, disembodied subculture seem chaotic, erratic, and even barbaric.

The real danger is that the misunderstanding has led to the removal of playtime, the mislabeling of recess as violent, and the total disregard that the children—not just the grown-ups—need recess. Japanese children have recess after each subject.[3] Education about the value of playtime as expressive culture is needed not merely for teacher's aides and lunch ladies but also teachers, principals, parents, and scholars.

Dan Olweus, an authority on bullying, notes the connection between stimulating play environments and a decline in bullying: "Bullying may become a way of making school life somewhat more exciting."[4] But the adult-framed structure not only ameliorates aggression but also exacerbates it. The removal of playtime only straitjackets expression and increases the likelihood of severe bullying.

Some observers have suggested that if commercials are invasive, eliminating recess offers one solution. Others have remarked on the distastefulness of games of physicality and danger, calling for their elimination. I am astounded by the simplicity of such suggestions. This argument for discarding the baby with the bathwater denies children the opportunity to synthesize and test their cultural and emotional realities through humor and through their bodies.

Children's physical intelligence is just beginning to be examined as a legitimate skill. The popularity of Howard Gardner's *Frames of Mind* (1983) in the education community and Robert and Michele Root-Bernstein's *Sparks of Genius* (1999) in the art community testify to the growing respect for bodily ways of knowing. But this new perspective has not yet been applied to public education or examined well in children's social environments. As more and more children play individually with objects and watch television and computer screens, social play is where children learn how to negotiate. Period.

What are teachers, parents, and other grown-ups to do? Advocate for children—all children, not just your own. Demand recess. Demand that children be allowed time to move their bodies. Demand art, music, and drama programs that allow children to express themselves. Assume that children need to express themselves as much as they need to take in information, and then watch, without judgment, the kinds of dramas the children express. To stop their expression of unpleasant sentiments does not make those feelings go away; rather, it simply displaces them.

Listen to your playground, and ask your children what things mean. Let the children have power at least in the one place in school that has traditionally been theirs. Let them decide what, where, and with what they play. Honor family and neighborhood traditions and have them bring them into the school. Give the children raw materials—sand, dirt, leaves, and chalk. Donate balls, ropes, and hoops to your schools. Educate children about what their words mean. Learn their words and their moves. Marvel at children's dreaminess. Try to remember what made your childhood vibrant.

Recognize children's needs for child-led socialization; adult-led activities, no matter how benevolent, will likely be unfulfilling. Gym is not play, although children may play during gym. Talk is not play, although a conversation may include playful banter. Individual exploration is related to play but usually only becomes playful when it is shared among equals.

Look for patterns, say the social scientists, and ask who is being served by the patterns in place. Pay attention to volatile transition times and spaces. Question what everyone assumes to be true. Ask why. Why is the school district's safety brochure called *Painting a Brighter Future* while art programs are being cut? How can basketball be the "antidrug" if there are no hoops? As a sticker on the Mill School's backboard urges, "Know Why."

Educate children about the agendas of the corporations that they encounter in popular culture. Have them be aware of the signs and symbols of their culture and engage them in discussions of exchange, power, and economy. Encourage the examination of popular arts and art history in the social sciences as a way to keep history meaningful, vibrant, and relevant to their lives. Challenge schools to be more playful.

Such organizations as the National Parent Teacher Association, the American Association for the Child's Right to Play, the American Playground Association, the Strong Museum of Play, and even the Cartoon Network say that they are ready to help with the preservation of recess.[5] Talk to your parent-teacher organization, your school board; see how you can organize your community. Organize an alternative school if you must.

For every ten grown-ups who did not understand the school yard there was one who did. As the aides were screaming for the children to line up and the children were sneaking one more turn in double-dutch, Ms. Gee, a fourth-grade teacher, slipped off her heels and jumped in. Delighted by their teacher's defiance, the girls turned faster and faster.

Ms. Gee squealed, her eyes crinkling along with her youthful smile, and got all the way to "Big Mac, Filet o' Fish, turnsies." Find the grown-ups in your community who understand play.

Brazilian playwright and activist Augusto Boal writes that "to transform something, first one must know it."[6] Document the recess battles and the children's cultural wrestlings.

In that spirit, I offer an invitation to hear the children's words in their own voices at www.recessbattles.com. No images of the children's faces appear, to protect their privacy, and no mention is made of the actual school where all this documentation took place. But there you will find more paintings, school yard activity maps, and some of these gamestories in their musical, lilting patter. These accounts were recorded live on the playground, so be prepared for a lot of conflicting noise. Your stories about your recess battles are welcome there.

Generalizations about childhood tend to fail and in turn fail to help children. Qualitative studies tend to be unrepeatable, and many scholars believe that such studies have questionable value. Janet Ward Schofield asks us to "reconceptualize generalizability" so that qualitative studies can be "translatable."[7] Schofield advises to study either the typical or the leading edge of change. The Mill School is both a typical concrete slab of a public school yard and a point of change in its diversity and its intersection with the market economy. It looks "typical," yet looks are deceiving. Although each concrete slab has its own stories, the stories of *all* urban, public elementary schools are also in each school yard, right next to the broken basketball hoop.

This project has focused on a specific place over time and makes no claims about children everywhere or about girl children, boy children, minority children, or poor children. It does however, point to the fluidity of racial, gendered, and class-related activity, making a case for the activity-based study of childhood. The children I studied have loudly and clearly demonstrated that as they playfully negotiate with each other in small groups, in large groups, with peers and institutions of power, they use a range of corresponding cultural texts and motifs. Recess serves as an artistic lab, a social meeting ground of ideas, where children do what they do. The children of the Mill School are still caught in their own transition, fighting gravity and wrestling giants.

I am
hard

POSTSCRIPT
Screaming Culture

December 9, 2004. I am back at the Mill School with new paintbrushes, india ink, and reams of paper. When I tell Ms. Headley's third-grade class that we will be doing art together, they say, "With paints?" When I answer "Yes," they wiggle and giggle and ooh and ahh. Ms. Headley has already somberly escorted them from the auditorium, coaxed them to use the bathroom, and inspected to make sure they are wearing their uniforms. She is the only teacher who has remained at the Mill School since I began the study in 1991.

The children are so hungry for the paint. Ms. Headley good-naturedly groans and admits they never get to paint. The students have hardly any paper. The principal wants posters for the walls but gives paper only to the "artistically talented," and it is not clear in Ms. Headley's bitterness if she thinks the principal is referring to the children or their teachers. I vow to bring more paper. We take so much for granted.

They experiment deliciously with their new brushes, bought with grant money from the university. They ask eagerly for more paper, more paper. When the india ink spills, they hold their breath, but I say, "When you do art, it's going to get messy." I go to clean up, and several children insist on helping: "I do this for my mom all the time. I do a lot of cleaning. I'm good at it."

I ask them to paint what they do at recess and how it makes them feel. They ask my permission for the littlest things. When one girl asks if she can turn over her slightly smudged paper, her classmate frowns, "You don't have to ask permission for that." One student asks if he has to hold his paper a certain way; I tell him he can hold it any way he likes. The teacher smiles approvingly at their self-control and says that they have to ask permission to do almost everything and then must do it a certain way. They are used to following instructions.

The class is evenly racially integrated—an anomaly, Ms. Headley tells me, because the school is no longer desegregated. One boy, a "chronic absentee," is again missing, probably because he got in trouble. "He was doing art," she says with a sarcastic smile, "in the auditorium, on the furniture." They have no money for drawing paper here, and I wonder about the connections and the irony of his punishment. The school doesn't even have scratch paper for math and spelling.

When I go to the girls' bathroom to clean the brushes, I see posters about self-control, ten feet high on the otherwise bland wall. "Count to 10." "Talk It Over." A wrinkled impressionist poster, also ten feet high, is the only thing on the next wall in the hallway. The walls have some book reports, in identical formats, and the hallway is a sickly yellow, fading, holding its breath.

I am thrilled by the children's expressiveness and saddened by their arbitrarily imposed limits. Their paintings are passionate, movement-filled social documents. Joy and struggle, dripping in black and white. One girl shyly gives me a sign that says, "First Place Teacher," and another says that instead of teaching college, I should teach third grade. Ms. Headley nods approvingly. As I leave, one girl says, "Come back in fourth grade." Another reminds me to take my bag of art supplies. I thank her and tell her that they belong to the class now, and Ms. Headley will keep the big bottle of ink and the new brushes and the extra paper for another time. "When you're feeling brave," I offer. "When I'm feeling brave," she laughs.

Outside, I hear:

NIKE NIKE WHO CAN DO THE NIKE?

SUI! NO RELAY!

Challenge Challenge

You gotta call RED, WHITE, and BLUE

Once your WHOLE BODY is OUT, you're OUT

WORK that BODY, ODDY, ODDY

Make SURE you DON'T hurt NOBODY

WE WORK WE WORK WE WORK

Criminal minded you been blinded

Looking for a shoe like mine can't find it

Reebok Walkers, You got Reebok Walkers?

R-E-E B-O-K. do your footsies the REEBOK way

Big MAC Filet o' FISH, FOOT and BOUNCE and HOP and

EEDIE IDIE ODIE

HERE comes the TEACHER with a

BIG FAT STICK

No running no talking no lifting

No eating no shoes off no touching

YOU GOT MY ENDS

Now take my goal post

APPENDIXES

GAMES CITED

All the Boys
Amoeba Tag
Bartman
Baseball
Basketball
Big Mac
Boogers
Boom Boom Tang
Boots
Build Up
Butt Like Mine
Catch
Chink
Chitty, Chitty, Bang, Bang
Criminal Minded
Dick against the Wall
D-I-S-H Choice
Down by the Banks
Down, Down Baby
Eedie Idie Odie
The Fighting Game
Firecracker, Firecracker
Fly Girl
Football
Freeze Tag
Girl Scout
Helicopter, Helicopter
Hey, DJ
Hollywood
Homicide

Hopscotch, Poison
I Work
Jack Be Nimble
Kitty Kat Bar
Leaf Games
Mailman, Mailman
Miniskirt
Nike, Nike
'N Sync, 'N Sync
Numbers
Pac Man
Play That Funky Music
Pump It Up
Punchinella
Reebok
Roaches
Roughhouse
Sand Games
Shoo, Shoo Sharida
Snag
Snow Games
Stoop Ball
Suicide
Swing, Swing, Swing (Rockin' Robin)
Tag
Telephone
Ups
Wall Ball

TRANSCRIPTIONS

Video Transcription, Wide Angle Footage, chapter 1
Video Transcription, Zoom Footage, chapter 1
Video Transcription, Hopscotch, chapter 3
Video Transcription, "Big Mac" Transcription 1, chapter 5
Video Transcription, "Big Mac" Transcription 2, chapter 5
Video Transcription, "Big Mac" Transcription 3, chapter 5
Video Transcription, "Big Mac" Transcription 4, chapter 5
Musical Transcription, "Pump It Up," chapter 6
Musical Transcription, "Shoo, Shoo Sharida," chapter 6
Musical Transcription, "Fly Girl," chapter 6
Musical Transcription, "Hollywood," chapter 6
Musical Transcription, "Telephone," chapter 6
Musical Transcription, I Work, chapter 6

NOTES

INTRODUCTION

1. See, e.g., Borman 1982; F. J. Brown 1939; Corsaro 1986, 2005; Damon 1977; Factor 2001; Mayall 2002; Ritchie and Koller 1964; Sutton-Smith et al. 1995.
2. DiGiullo 2001.
3. Axline 1947; Erikson 1950, 1975; M. Klein 1932/1975; Winnicott 1971; see also Piaget 1962, 1965.
4. Turner 1982.
5. For explanations of the significance of performance in context in folklore study, see Bauman 1986; Ben-Amos 1972; Glassie 1989. For a precursor in sociology, see Goffman 1959.
6. Handelman 1990.
7. In 1991, under the desegregation mandate, the school was approximately 50 percent white and 50 percent black. Because the Mill School was a desegregation magnet school, African American children were bused in from neighborhoods with less desirable schools. By 2004, the U.S. Supreme Court had officially dismantled the desegregation program, and in its place was No Child Left Behind. Individual children, regardless of race, could apply to go to the Mill School (or another school of choice) if they could demonstrate that their local school had poorer scores than their school of choice. In 2004, the Mill School was 60 percent black, 38 percent white, and 2 percent Asian and Latino.
8. According to the International Playground Association, a recess advocacy group, 40 percent of American schools have removed or are in the process of removing recess. The association also documents the use of recess withdrawal as a form of punishment. See www .ipausa.org.
9. Blatchford 1998; Cavallo 1981; King 1987; Mead 1999; Pellegrini 1995; Sutton-Smith 1997; see also Jemie 2003; Jones and Hawes 1972; Thorne 1993.
10. L. Cohen 2003; Kline 1993; Ritzer 1998; Schlosser 2002; Schor 2004; see also Goldman and Papson 1998; Jackson and Andrews 2005; Kellner 2001; Kenway and Bullen 2001; Kincheloe 1997; Lasn 1999; Lears 1988; Vanderbilt 1998.
11. See, e.g., Erikson 1950, 1975; Winnicott 1971.
12. See e.g., Blacking 1967; Lancy 1996, 2002; Schwartzman 1978.

13. Willis 1990, 19.
14. Baker and Heyning 2004; Bourdieu and Passerson 2000; Hollingsworth and Boyes 1997; Schmookler 1993.
15. Willis 1990, 17–18.
16. Willis 1977 is an education classic; see similarly Foley 1994. For more on the complexities of dialectics, see Calabrese 2004; Engels 1883/1940.
17. See Sutton-Smith 1978, 1989, 1997.
18. According to Gloria Levitas, a former student of Mead's, she believed that playgrounds were excellent sites for the analysis of both psychology and culture and assigned ethnographic playground studies in class. Levitas shared this recollection with me at the 2001 meeting of the Society for Psychological Anthropology at Queens College.
19. LeVine 1974; Wallace 1961; Whiting 1963; Whiting and Edwards 1988. For a fine introduction to the Frankfurt School, see Kline, Dyer-Witherford, and dePeuter 2003; Nealon and Irr 2002; Wiggershaus 1994.
20. Arendt 1969; Bateson 1972; Benjamin 1996. Although Bateson made play a central subject in his research, Benjamin addressed it obliquely through his study of art, games, and toys. According to Arendt, for Benjamin, "the size of an object was in inverse ratio to its significance" (1969, 11).
21. See Erikson 1950; Bateson 1972.
22. See Birdwhistell 1970; Erickson 1990, 2004; Kendon 1990.
23. For a classic discussion of emic (inside) knowledge and etic (outside) knowledge, see Pike 1954.
24. See Ball 1990; Cladis 1999; Olssen 1999; Popkewitz and Brennan 1998.
25. See Lareau 2003.
26. Opie and Opie 1968, 1969, 1988.
27. Sutton-Smith 1972a, 1976, 1981b.
28. Jemie 2003.
29. See also Bronner 1988; Knapp and Knapp 1976; Newell 1883/1963.
30. See Schwartzman 1978; Eifermann 1971; Thorne 1993; see also Lanclos 2003. Although there seems to be new interest in studies about play, culture, and schooling, some, including Lewis 2003, are about schooling and race rather than about the school yard per se. For studies of African American children at play, see Brady 1975; Eckhardt 1975; Jemie 2003; Jones and Hawes 1972.
31. Piaget 1965, 1. For more on Piaget, see chapter 2.

CHAPTER 1

1. Bateson 1972.
2. Aldis 1975.
3. Pellegrini 1995, 2005; see also Boulton and Smith 1989; Fagen 1981; Groos 1898. For adult misperceptions of play fighting, see Conner 1989.
4. Bourdieu 1990; Bourdieu and Passerson 2000.
5. See Goffman 1967. For the significance of facial gestures in mock violent play, see also Kendon 1990.

6. Classics in transition study include Bianchi 1986; Y. Cohen 1963; Fried and Fried 1980; Goffman 1974; Goodwin and Goodwin 1990; Helve 1986; Pentikainen 1986; Turner 1982, 1987; van Gennep 1960; Winnicott 1971; Young 1965.

7. For more on the connection between crowding and violent behavior, see Hartup and Laursen 1993, viii.

8. On the "hidden transcripts of rebellion," see Scott 1990. My favorite is Scott's epigraph: "When the great lord passes the wise peasant bows deeply and silently farts" (Ethiopian Proverb).

CHAPTER 2

1. Paley 1988; Pitcher and Prelinger 1963; Sutton-Smith 1981a; Winner and Gardner 1979. For a wonderful collection of narratives by six-year-olds, see Kalliala 2006.

2. Cowie 1983; Gould and Coyne 1945; Mearnes 1958.

3. See Coles 1986a, 1986b; Kozol 2000, 2005. For more on the anthropology of childhood, see Scheper-Hughes and Sargent 1998; Schwartzman 2001. See Kirshenblatt-Gimblett 1976 and Stewart 1978 for more on nonsense. Stewart 1978 sees nonsense as something "out of place" that shakes us into seeing connections that might have been too strange to recognize without the mask of silliness.

4. Gale 1996; Gooding-Williams 1993; Jacobs 2000; Khalifah 1992.

5. Bakhtin 1981; Stallybrass and White 1986.

6. See Axline 1947; Erikson 1950, 1975; Klein 1932/1975; Winnicott 1971.

7. Goffman 1959; Singer and Singer 1990; Vygotsky 1978. For more on the notion of a game/play/story continuum, see Abrahams 1976; Jemie 2003.

8. Piaget 1962, 179.

9. Erikson 1950, 213, 211.

10. Freud 1907, 143–44, 149.

11. Hobson 1988; Foulkes 1999; see also Domhoff 2003.

12. Shulman and Stroumsa 1999, 6.

13. Erikson 1950, 230. For more on the connection between playing and dreaming, see also Singer and Singer 1990; Sutton-Smith 1997.

14. Sutton-Smith 1997, 61.

15. Domhoff 2003, 168, 145.

16. Opie 1993/2001, xii.

17. Bruner 1986, 148.

18. In the 1970s, folklore study turned from the study of history and culture to the study of culture in performance—the study of artistic communication in small groups. Instead of tracing the oldest version of a ballad or folktale, folklorists became concerned with the dynamics of the telling, the ethnomusicology of its recording. But even after the performance revolution, issues of quantity were rarely addressed. See Ben Amos 1972.

19. For games as national identity, see Bronner 1988; Knapp and Knapp 1976; Newell 1883/1963; Opie and Opie 1968, 1969. For games as ethnic or regional identity, see Eckhardt 1975; Eifermann 1971; Gaunt 2006; Jemie 2003; Jones and Hawes 1972; Schwartzman 1978. For games as international equivalents, see Arleo 2001; J. Bishop and Curtis 2001; Butler 1989. The listing of many variants sometimes but not always suggests popularity.

20. For the clearest presentation of these two opposite viewpoints, cf. Glassie 1989, 1999; Goldstein 1964.

CHAPTER 3

1. Piaget 1965.
2. Vygotsky 1978.
3. For a general introduction to negotiation as a process, see Lewicki, Barry, and Saunders 2007; Strauss 1978.
4. See Tylor 1971.
5. Piaget (1962) has called this balancing disequilibration, a process of assimilation and accommodation of inside and outside needs. For Vygotsky (1978), play, like all growing, occurs within the tension of a virtual zone of proximal development; we reach for a level of complexity just beyond our current skill level. The process helps us grow.
6. Brewster 1953.
7. For more on the ritual of counting out, see Goldstein 1971.
8. Piaget 1965, 77; for more on legality disagreements at play, see Ariel 2002.
9. See Opie and Opie 1969, 4; Bronner 1988; Knapp and Knapp 1976, 6.
10. Newell 1883/1963, 188.
11. Goffman 1959, 1974.
12. For more on the recent discussion about passivity in girls' development, see L. M. Brown and Gilligan 1992; Gilligan, Ward, and Taylor 1988. I prefer to think of passivity as a lost opportunity rather than a stage. For a fine study of gender separation on playgrounds, see Thorne 1993. I question the wide-brush approach to gender patterns and prefer the ethnographic description of specific activity in a specific location.
13. For other examples of how children toy with space, see Armitage 2001.

CHAPTER 4

1. Kline 1993 makes this point. As much as children are bombarded with commercial scripts, they are not robots.
2. The challenger does a complex double-dutch pattern of her choice. Each jumper must repeat the pattern exactly and then extend it, if possible. This was a favorite among the most advanced jumpers in 1991, 1999, and 2004. Those who were holding the ends of the rope often practiced their moves silently on the side. "Hey Consolation" has pieces of the African American classic "Hambone, Hambone, Where You Been." The stylized counting of "2, 4, 6, 8, 10, hop" is also recorded in Abrahams 1963.
3. Gaunt 2006.
4. Jemie 2003; Knapp and Knapp 1976.
5. Bronner 1988.
6. Jemie 2003.
7. Knapp and Knapp 1976.
8. Knapp and Knapp 1976.
9. Bourdieu 1990, 159.
10. For more on Channel 1, see Kenway and Bullen 2001; Lasn 1999.

11. For more on Project PLAY, see Goldman and Papson 1998. For more on McDonald's marketing to children and its charitable endeavors, see Kenway and Bullen 2001; Kincheloe 1997; Ritzer 1998; Schor 2004.
12. Gender, race, and class used to be examined separately, but scholars now see those factors as intertwined. See Gaine and George 1999; Weis 1988. For excellent examples of scholarship focusing on race and class in childhood study, see Lareau 2003; Willie 1983.
13. Vanderbilt 1998, 71.
14. Goldman and Papson 1998, 169.
15. Appadurai 1986, 56. For more on the "cultural contradictions of capitalism," see also Bell 1976.
16. Lears 1988, 133.
17. West 2004, 179.
18. For a critique of the linking of African American culture with poverty and the angst of hip-hop, see Jeffries 1992; Kitwana 2002; Toop 1984/1991. For more on the changing role of women in hip hop, see Gaunt 2006; T. Rose 1994. For Langston Hughes's commentary on whites' misunderstanding and appropriation of jazz, see Hughes and Bontemps 1958, 609.
19. Schor 2004, 50.
20. West 1992, 40–41.

CHAPTER 5

1. Bell 1976.
2. Willis 1977.
3. Kozol 2005.
4. Freud 1930, 25.
5. Lareau 2003.
6. This and the following two quotations come from the "Recess" section of the International Playground Association Web site, www.ipausa.org/recess.html. The association is the most vocal institutional advocate of "children's right to play."
7. Most books dealing with children's play rights focus on early childhood. See Clements and Fiorentino 2004. The National Association for Educators of Young Children also advocates play; no parallel with power exists for adults working with children older than five in this country.
8. Grinde 2002.
9. Erikson 1950, 211.
10. Seligman 1995, 2002.
11. Foucault 1977, 25–26; see also Honneth 1991.
12. Dickens 1873.

CHAPTER 6

1. Also recorded in Abrahams 1963.
2. Also appears in Knapp and Knapp 1976.
3. Also appears in Abrahams 1969b. He recorded it personally in Philadelphia in 1963.

4. *Late* has a double meaning here. When someone missed her jumping cue, the girls would chant, "Late, late, late." A KitKat is a chocolate candy bar. Jemie 2003 lists a similar game called "Be on Time."

5. Newell 1883/1963.

6. See Seeger 1955/1997; also cited in Merrill-Mirsky 1988.

7. Also cited in Gaunt 2006; Jemie 2003; Merrill-Mirsky 1988.

8. Also cited in Jemie 2003.

9. Partially cited in Abrahams 1969b; Brady 1975; Jemie 2003; Merrill-Mirsky 1988.

10. Cited in Merrill-Mirsky 1988.

11. Merrill-Mirsky 1988. Pete Seeger recorded a version of this song known as "The Foolish Frog," but it is nestled in a different tale. See Seeger 1955/1997.

12. Jemie 2003; Jones and Hawes 1972; Opie and Opie 1988; Sutton-Smith, 1981b.

13. Fine 2003; Malone 1996.

14. For step instruction and the wisdom behind the genre, see Jones and Hawes 1972; see also *Films* 2003.

15. Jemie 2003, 51.

16. For more on ritual insults, see Abrahams 1969b, 1972; Labov 1972; Percelay, Ivey, and Dweck 1994; Toop 1984/1991; Whitten and Szwed 1970.

CHAPTER 7

1. Williams 1976; see also Bennett, Grossberg, and Morris 2005.

2. Abrahams 2005.

3. Pike 1954.

4. See Opie and Opie 1968, 1969 (Britain); Newell 1883/1963 (United States); Sutton-Smith 1981b (New Zealand).

5. E.g., Butler 1989.

6. Abrahams 1963; Anderson 1978; Liebow 1966; D. Rose 1975; Whyte 1943. For an excellent more recent example, see Duneier 1999.

7. For a larger discussion of play's attributes, see chapter 8.

8. The classic text on pregame ceremonies and counting out is Goldstein 1971. Once a staple of playground games, such counting out has become less frequent as a consequence of the interference of grown-ups intending to save the children time.

9. For more on laughter as a compound gesture, see Morris 1977.

10. Boal 2002, 48. In the words of playwright Augusto Boal, "A bodily movement is a thought" (2002, 49).

11. On boys' play fighting, see Pellegrini 2005; Thorne 1993.

12. Kozol 2005.

CHAPTER 8

1. See Sutton-Smith 1997.

2. On animal play, see Fagen 1981. Sutton-Smith describes attributes of play in several of his works, esp. 1997.

3. Bateson (1972) is most associated with the metamessages of play; see also Sutton-Smith 1997.

4. See Benjamin 1996; Erikson 1950, 1975; Piaget 1962, 1965; Willis 1977, 1990.

5. See, in order, Vygotsky 1978; Goffman 1959, 1967, 1974; Bourdieu 1990.

6. Swartz 1997, 126, 189–90. Swartz clarifies the differences between Bourdieu's perspective and those of Foucault, Althusser, Goffman, and Marxist doctrine (121, 89).

7. For more on the transforming quality of play, see Schwartzman 1978.

8. For more on paradox and communication, see Bateson 1979; Smith and Berg 1987; Tannen 2007.

9. See Pellegrini 2005. Pellegrini says, "If recess does indeed interfere with children's learning, then it should be minimized. Correspondingly, if it facilitates learning and achievement, it should be supported and possibly expanded" (2005, 141). See also the Web site for the Strong Museum of Play, www.museumofplay.org.

10. Henig 2008.

11. Blatchford 1998 quoted in Pellegrini and Blatchford 2000, 72.

12. Pellegrini 1995, 184; see also Sluckin 1981.

13. Barros, Silver, and Stein 2009.

14. Parker-Pope 2009.

15. Henig 2008.

16. Factor 2001.

17. Willis 1990, 11–12.

18. Salen and Zimmerman offer an elegant definition: "Play is free movement in a more rigid structure" (2004, 304). I would add that it is through exaggerated movement that play exists. Play is exaggeration in speed or size, time or space, effort or shape. It is not just within a framework. It is dialogic, negotiated. I play with someone. I toy with this thing. I am game. Play is exaggerated negotiation.

CONCLUSION

1. Bird 2003, 201. For more on chaos theory, see Butz 1997; Gleick 1988; Goerner 1994; Grebogi and Yorke 1997; Kaye 1993; Lorenz 1993; Makishima 2001; Sardar and Abrams 1999.

2. Shore 1996; on the anthropology of children's space, see Olwig and Gullov 2003.

3. Although different Japanese schools offer different types of breaks, several Web sites and educator journals mention Japan's frequent recess periods as an alternative model. See Cromwell 1998/2006. See also the International Playground Association Web site, www .ipausa.org.

4. Olweus 1993, 71.

5. R. Bishop 2009.

6. Boal 2002, 209. Boal is the creator of the Theater of the Oppressed, which uses games to help communities face forms of localized oppression. In essence, the school yard can be seen as a living model, a precursor of such theater.

7. Schofield 2007, 186, 187.

BIBLIOGRAPHY

Abrahams, R. D. 1963. Some jump rope rhymes from South Philadelphia. *Keystone Folklore Quarterly* 8:3–15.

Abrahams, R. D. 1969a. *Jump rope rhymes: A dictionary*. Austin: University of Texas Press for the American Folklore Society.

Abrahams, R. D. 1969b. *Positively black*. Englewood Cliffs, NJ: Prentice Hall.

Abrahams, R. D. 1972. Joking: The training of the man of words in talking broad. In T. Kochman, ed., *Rappin' and stylin' out: communication in urban black America*, 215–40. Urbana: University of Illinois Press.

Abrahams, R. D. 1976. The complex relations of simple forms. In D. Ben Amos, ed., *Folklore genres*, 193–214. Austin: University of Texas Press.

Abrahams, R. D. 2005. *Everyday life: A poetics of vernacular practices*. Philadelphia: University of Pennsylvania Press.

Aldis, O. 1975. *Play fighting*. New York: Academic Press.

Alisch, L. M., S. Azizighanbari, and M. Bargfeldt. 1997. Dynamics of children's friendships. In R. A. Eve, S. Horsfall, and M. E. Lee, eds. *Chaos, complexity and sociology: Myths, models, and theories*, 163–81. Thousand Oaks, CA: Sage.

Anderson, E. 1978. *A place on the corner*. Chicago: University of Chicago Press.

Anderson, E. 1999. *Code of the street: Decency, violence, and the moral life of the inner city*. New York: Norton.

Appadurai, A. 1986. *The social life of things: Commodities in cultural perspective*. Cambridge: Cambridge University Press.

Arendt, H. 1969. Introduction: Walter Benjamin, 1892–1940. In W. Benjamin, *Illuminations*, 1–58. New York: Schocken.

Ariel, S. 2002. *Children's imaginative play: A visit to wonderland*. Westport, CT: Praeger.

Arleo, A. 2001. The saga of Susie: The dynamics of an international handclapping game. In J. Bishop and M. Curtis, eds., *Play today in the primary school playground*, 115–32. Buckingham: Open University Press.

Armitage, M. 2001. The ins and outs of school playground play: children's use of "play places." In J. Bishop and M. Curtis, eds., *Play today in the primary school playground*, 37–57. Buckingham: Open University Press.

Asante, M. F., and A. Mazama. 2005. *Encyclopedia of black studies.* Thousand Oaks, CA: Sage.

Axline, V. 1947. *Play therapy: The inner dynamics of childhood.* Boston: Houghton, Mifflin.

Baker, B. M., and K. E. Heyning. 2004. *Dangerous coagulations? The Uses of Foucault in the study of education.* New York: Lang.

Bakhtin, M. 1981. *The dialogic imagination.* Austin: University of Texas Press.

Ball, S. J. 1990. *Foucault and education: Disciplines and knowledge.* London: Routledge.

Barros, R. M., E. J. Silver, and R. Stein. 2009. School recess and group classroom behavior. *Pediatrics* 123:431–36.

Bateson, G. 1972. *Steps to an ecology of mind.* New York: Ballantine.

Bateson, G. 1979. *Mind and nature.* New York: Dutton.

Bauman, R. 1986. *Story, performance, and event: Contextual studies of oral narrative.* Cambridge: Cambridge University Press.

Bell, D. 1976. *The cultural contradictions of capitalism.* New York: Basic.

Ben Amos, D. 1972. Toward a definition of folklore in context. In A. Paredes and R. Bauman, eds., *Toward new perspectives in folklore,* 5–15. Austin: University of Texas Press.

Benjamin, W. 1996. Old forgotten children's books. In M. Bullock and M. W. Jennings, eds., *Walter Benjamin: Selected writings,* vol. 1, *1913–1926,* 407–13. Cambridge: Harvard University Press.

Bennett, T., L. Grossberg, and M. Morris. 2005. *New keywords: A revised vocabulary of culture and society.* Malden, MA: Blackwell.

Beresin, A. R. 1995. Double dutch and double cameras: Studying the transmission of culture in an urban school yard. In B. Sutton-Smith, et al., eds. *Children's folklore: A source book,* 75–91. New York: Garland.

Beresin, A. R. 1996. "Sui" generis: Mock violence in an urban school yard. *Children's Folklore Review* 18:25–35.

Beresin, A. R. 2004. School power, recess play, and the timing of recess violence. In M. Anderson, ed., *The cultural shaping of violence.* West Lafayette, IN: Purdue University Press.

Bertrand, M. 1976. Rough-and-tumble in stumptails. In J. S. Bruner, A. Jolly, and K. Sylva, eds., *Play —Its role in development and evolution,* 320–27. New York: Basic Books.

Beruglia, C. S., and V. Franco. 2005. *Nonlinearity, chaos and complexity: The dynamics of natural and social sciences.* Oxford: Oxford University Press.

Bianchi, U. 1986. Some observations on the typology of passage. In U. Bianchi, ed., *Transition rites: Cosmic, social and individual order,* 45–59. Rome: Bretschneider.

Binmore, K. G., L. Samuelson, and R. Vaughan. 1994. *Musical chairs: Modelling noisy evolution.* London: University College London.

Bird, R. J. 2003. *Chaos and life: Complexity and order in evolution and thought.* New York: Columbia University Press.

Birdwhistell, R. 1970. *Kinesics and Context: Essays on body motion communication.* Philadelphia: University of Pennsylvania Press.

Bishop, J., and M. Curtis. 2001. *Play today in the primary school playground: Life, learning, and creativity.* Buckingham: Open University Press.

Bishop, R. 2009. *When play was play: Why pick-up games matter.* Albany: State University of New York Press.

Blacking, J. 1967. *Venda children's songs.* Johannesburg: Witwatersrand University Press.

Blatchford, P. 1998. *Social life in school: Pupils experience of breaktime and recess from 7 to 16 years.* London: Falmer.

Blurton-Jones, N. 1976. Rough-and-tumble among nursery school children. In J. S. Bruner, A. Jolly, and K. Sylva, eds., *Play—Its role in development and evolution,* 352–63. New York: Basic Books.

Boal, A. 2002. *Games for actors and non-actors.* London: Routledge.

Borman, K. M. 1982. *The social life of children in a changing society.* Hillsdale, NJ: Erlbaum.

Boulton, M., and P. K. Smith. 1989. Issues in the study of children's rough-and-tumble play. In M. Bloch and A. D. Pellegrini, eds., *The ecological context of children's play,* 57–83. Norwood, NJ: Ablex.

Bourdieu, P. 1990. *In other words: Essays towards a reflexive sociology.* Stanford: Stanford University Press.

Bourdieu, P., and J.-C. Passerson. 2000. *Reproduction in education, society, and culture.* London: Sage.

Brady, M. 1975. "This little lady's gonna boogaloo": Elements of socialization in the play of black girls. In R. Bauman, ed., *Black girls at play: Folkloric perspectives on child development,* 1–56. Austin, TX: Southwest Educational Development Laboratory.

Brewster, P. G. 1953. *American nonsinging games.* Norman: University of Oklahoma Press.

Bronner, S. J. 1988. *American children's folklore.* Little Rock, AR: August House.

Brown, F. J. 1939. *The sociology of childhood.* New York: Prentice-Hall.

Brown, L. M., and C. Gilligan. 1992. *Meeting at the crossroads: Women's psychology and girls' development.* Cambridge: Harvard University Press.

Bruner, J. 1986. *Actual minds, possible worlds.* Cambridge: Harvard University Press.

Butler, F. 1989. *Skipping around the world: The ritual nature of folk rhymes.* Hamden, CT: Library Professional.

Butz, M. R. 1997. *Chaos and complexity: Implication for psychological theory and practice.* Washington, D.C.: Taylor and Francis.

Calabrese, A. 2004. Toward a political economy of culture. In A. Calabrese and C. Sparks, eds., *Toward a political economy of culture: Capitalism and communication in the twenty-first century,* 1–12. Lanham, MD: Rowman and Littlefield.

Cavallo, D. 1981. *Muscles and morals: Organized playgrounds and urban reform, 1880–1920.* Philadelphia: University of Pennsylvania Press.

Cladis, M. S. 1999. *Durkheim and Foucault: Perspectives on education and punishment.* Oxford: Durkheim.

Clements, R., and L. Fiorentino. 2004. *The child's right to play: A global approach.* Westport, CT: Praeger.

Cohen, L. 2003. *A consumer's republic: The politics of mass consumption in postwar America.* New York: Knopf.

Cohen, Y. 1963. *The transition from childhood to adolescence: Legal systems and taboos.* Chicago: Aldine.

Coles, R. 1986a. *The moral life of children.* Boston: Atlantic Monthly Press.

Coles, R. 1986b. *The political life of children.* Boston: Atlantic Monthly Press.

Conner, K. 1989. Aggression: Is it in the eye of the beholder? *Play and Culture* 2:213–17.

Corsaro, W. 1986. Routines in peer culture. In J. Cook-Gumperz, W. Corsaro, and J. Streeck, eds., *Children's worlds and children's language,* 231–52. The Hague: Mouton de Gruyter.

Corsaro, W. 2005. *The sociology of childhood*. Thousand Oaks, CA: Pine Forge.

Cowie, H. 1983. *Development of children's imaginative writing*. New York: St. Martin's.

Crombie, J. W. 1886. History of the game of hopscotch. *Journal of the Anthropological Institute of Great Britain and Ireland* 15:403–4.

Cromwell, S. 1998/2006. Should Schools Take a Break from Recess? *Education World*, September 1.

Damon, W. 1977. *The social world of the child*. San Francisco: Jossey-Bass.

Dickens, C. 1873. *Hard times*. In *The works of Charles Dickens*. New York: New York Book Concern.

Domhoff, G. W. 2003. *The scientific study of dreams: Neural networks, cognitive development, and content analysis*. Washington, D.C.: American Psychological Association.

Dorson, R. M. 1956. *American Negro folktales*. Greenwich, CT: Fawcett.

DiGiullo, R. 2001. *Educate, medicate, or litigate: What teachers, parents, and administrators must do about student behavior*. Thousand Oaks, CA: Corwin.

Duneier, M. 1999. *Sidewalk*. New York: Farrar, Straus, and Giroux.

Eckhardt, R. 1975. From handclap to line play. In R. Bauman, ed., *Black girls at play: Folkloric perspectives on child development*, 57–103. Austin, TX: Southwest Educational Development Laboratory.

Eifermann, R. 1971. *Determinants of children's game styles: On free play in a "disadvantaged" and in an "advantaged" school*. Jerusalem: Israel Academy of Sciences and Humanities.

Elliot, E., and L. D. Kiel. 1997. Nonlinear dynamics, complexity, and public policy: Use, misuse, and applicability. In R. A. Eve, S. Horsfal, and M. E. Lee, eds., *Chaos, complexity and sociology: Myths, models, and theories*, 64–78. Thousand Oaks, CA: Sage.

Engels, F. 1883/1940. *Dialectics of nature*. New York: International.

Erickson, F. 1990. Qualitative methods. In R. L. Linn and F. Erickson, eds., *Quantitative methods qualitative methods*, 77–187. New York: Macmillan.

Erickson, F. 2004. *Talk and social theory: Ecologies of speaking and listening in everyday life*. Cambridge: Polity.

Erikson, E. 1950. *Childhood and society*. New York: Norton.

Erikson, E. 1975. *Studies of play*. New York: Arno.

Factor, J. 2001. Three myths about children's folklore. In J. C. Bishop and M. Curtis, eds., *Play today in the elementary school yard*, 24–37. Buckingham: Open University Press.

Fagen, R. 1981. *Animal play behavior*. New York: Oxford University Press.

The Films of Bess Lomax Hawes. 2003. Media-Generation.com.

Fine, E. C. 2003. *Soulstepping: African American step shows*. Urbana: University of Illinois Press.

Foley, D. 1994. *Learning capitalist culture: Deep in the heart of Tejas*. Philadelphia: University of Pennsylvania Press.

Foucault, M. 1977. *Discipline and punish: The birth of the prison*. New York: Pantheon.

Foulkes, D. 1999. *Children's dreaming and the development of consciousness*. Cambridge: Harvard University Press.

Freud, S. 1907. Creative writers and day-dreaming. In E. S. Person, et al., eds., *On Freud's "Creative writers and day-dreaming,"* 143–49. New Haven: Yale University Press, 1995.

Freud, S. 1930. *Civilization and its discontents*. New York: Cape and Smith.

Fried, M. N., and M. H. Fried. 1980. *Transitions: Four rituals in eight cultures.* New York: Norton.

Gaine, C., and R. George. 1999. *Gender, "race," and class in schooling: A new introduction.* London: Falmer.

Gale, D. 1996. *Understanding urban unrest: From Reverend King to Rodney King.* Thousand Oaks, CA: Sage.

Gardner, H. 1983. *Frames of mind: The theory of multiple intelligences.* New York: Basic Books.

Gates, H. L., Jr. 2002. The talking book. In H. Dodson, ed., *Jubilee: The emergence of African-American culture,* 163–67. Washington, D.C.: National Geographic.

Gaunt, K. 2006. *The games black girls play: From double-dutch to hip-hop.* New York: New York University Press.

Gilligan, C., J. Ward, and J. Taylor. 1988. *Mapping the moral domain: A contribution of women's thinking to psychological theory and education.* Cambridge: Harvard University Press.

Glassie, H. H. 1989. *The spirit of folk art.* New York: Abrams, in association with the Museum of New Mexico, Santa Fe.

Glassie, H. H. 1999. *Material culture.* Bloomington: Indiana University Press.

Gleick, J. 1988. *Chaos: Making a new science.* New York: Penguin.

Goerner, S. J. 1994. *Chaos and the evolving ecological universe.* Langhorne, PA: Gordon and Breach.

Goffman, E. 1959. *The presentation of self in everyday life.* Garden City, NY: Doubleday.

Goffman, E. 1967. *Interaction ritual: Essays on face-to-face behavior.* Chicago: Aldine.

Goffman, E. 1974. *Frame analysis.* Cambridge: Harvard University Press.

Goldman, R., and S. Papson. 1998. *Nike culture.* Thousand Oaks, CA: Sage.

Goldstein, K. S. 1964. *A guide for fieldworkers in folklore.* Hatboro, PA: Folklore Associates.

Goldstein, K. S. 1971. Strategy in counting out: An ethnographic folklore field study. In E. M. Avedon and B. Sutton-Smith, eds., *The Study of Games,* 167–78. New York: Wiley.

Gooding-Williams, R. 1993. *Reading Rodney King, reading urban uprising.* New York: Routledge.

Goodwin, C., and M. H. Goodwin. 1990. Interstitial argument. In A. Grimshaw, ed., *Conflict talk: Sociolinguistic investigations of arguments in conversations,* 85–117. Cambridge: Cambridge University Press.

Gould, K. M., and J. Coyne. 1945. *Young voice: A quarter century of high school student writing selected from scholastic awards.* New York: Harper.

Grebogi, C., and J. A. Yorke. 1997. *The impact of chaos on science and society.* Tokyo: United Nations University Press.

Grinde, B. 2002. *Darwinian happiness: Evolution as a guide for living and understanding human behavior.* Princeton, NJ: Darwin.

Groos, K. 1898. *The play of animals.* New York: Appleton.

Handelman, D. 1990. *Models and mirrors: Toward an anthropology of public events.* Cambridge: Cambridge University Press.

Hartup, W. W., and B. Laursen. 1993. Conflict and context in peer relations. In C. Hart, ed., *Children on playgrounds: Research perspectives and applications,* 44–84. Albany: State University of New York Press.

Helve, H. 1986. Youth culture, transition rites. In U. Bianchi, ed., *Transition rites: Cosmic, social, and individual order,* 227–33. Rome: Bretschneider.

Henig, R. M. 2008. Taking play seriously: What can science tell us about why kids run and jump. *New York Times Magazine*, February 17, 38–45, 60, 75.

Hobson, J. A. 1988. *The dreaming brain*. New York: Basic Books.

Hollingsworth, J. K., and T. R. Boyes. 1997. *Contemporary capitalism: The embeddedness of institutions*. Cambridge: Cambridge University Press.

Honneth, A. 1991. *The critique of power: Reflective stages in a critical social theory*. Cambridge: MIT Press.

Hughes, L., and A. Bontemps. 1958. *The book of Negro folklore*. New York: Dodd, Mead.

Humphreys, A., and P. K. Smith. 1984. Rough-and tumble in preschool and playground. In P. K. Smith, ed., *Play in animals and humans*, 241–70. London: Blackwell.

Jackson, S. F., and D. L. Andrews. 2005. *Sport, culture and advertising: Identities, commodities, and the power of repression*. London: Routledge.

Jacobs, R. N. 2000. *Race, media, and the crisis of civil society: From Watts to Rodney King*. Cambridge: Cambridge University Press.

Jeffries, J. 1992. Toward a redefinition of the urban: The collision of culture. In D. Dent, ed., *Black popular culture*, 153–63. Seattle, WA: Bay Press.

Jemie, O. 2003. *Yo' mama! New raps, toasts, dozens, jokes and children's rhymes from urban black America*. New Brunswick: Rutgers University Press.

Jones, B., and B. L. Hawes. 1972. *Step it down: Games, plays, songs, and stories from the Afro-American heritage*. Athens: University of Georgia Press.

Kalliala, M. 2006. *Play culture in a changing world*. Maidenhead: Open University Press.

Kaye, B. 1993. *Chaos and complexity: Discovering the surprising patterns of science and technology*. Weinheim: VCH.

Kellner, D. 2001. The sports spectacle, Michael Jordan, and Nike: Unholy Alliance? In D. L. Andrews, ed., *Michael Jordan, Inc.: Corporate sport, media culture, and late modern America*. Albany: State University of New York Press.

Kendon, A. 1990. *Conducting interaction: Patterns of behavior in focused encounters*. Cambridge: Cambridge University Press.

Kenway, J., and E. Bullen. 2001, *Consuming children: Education, entertainment, advertising*. Buckingham: Open University Press.

Khalifah, H. K., ed. 1992. *Rodney King and the L.A. rebellion: Analysis and commentary by thirteen independent black writers*. Hampton, VA: U.B. and U.S. Communications Systems.

Kincheloe, J. L. 1997. McDonald's, power, and children: Ronald McDonald aka Ray Kroc does it all for you. In S. R. Steinburst and J. L. Kincheloe, eds., *Kinderculture: The corporate construction of childhood*, 120–49. Boulder, CO: Westview.

King, N. A. 1987. Elementary school play: theory and research. In J. H. Block and N. R. King, eds., *School play: A source book*, 143–66. New York: Garland.

Kirshenblatt-Gimblett, B. 1976. *Speech play: Research and resources for studying linguistic creativity*. Philadelphia: University of Pennsylvania Press.

Kitwana, B. 2002. *The hip-hop generation: Young blacks and the crisis in African American culture*. New York: Basic Books.

Klein, M. 1932/1975. *The psycho-analysis of children*. Trans. A. Strachey. London: Hogarth.

Kline, S. 1993. *Out of the garden: Toys, TV, and children's culture in the age of marketing*. London: Verso.

Kline, S., N. Dyer-Witherford, and G. dePeuter. 2003. *Digital play: The interaction of technology, culture, and marketing.* Montreal: McGill-Queen's University Press.

Knapp, M., and H. Knapp. 1976. *One potato, two potato: The folklore of American children.* New York: Norton.

Kozol, J. 2000. *Ordinary resurrections: Children in the years of hope.* New York: Crown.

Kozol, J. 2005. *Shame of the nation: The restoration of apartheid schooling in America.* New York: Crown.

Labov, B. 1972. Rules for ritual insult. In T. Kochman, ed., *Rappin' and stylin' out: Communication in urban black America,* 265–314. Urbana: University of Illinois Press.

Lanclos, D. 2003. *At play in Belfast: Children's folklore and identities in Northern Ireland.* New Brunswick: Rutgers University Press.

Lancy, D. 1996. *Playing on the mother ground: Cultural routines for children's development.* New York: Guilford.

Lancy, D. 2002. Cultural constraints on children's play. In J. L. Roopnarine, ed., *Conceptual, social-cognitive, and contextual issues in the fields of play,* 4:53–63. Westport, CT: Ablex.

Lareau, D. 2003. *Unequal childhoods: Race, class, and family life.* Berkeley: University of California Press.

Lasn, K. 1999. *Culture jam: how to reverse America's suicidal consumer binge and why we must.* New York: Quill.

Lears, J. 1988. Packaging the folk: Tradition and amnesia in American advertising, 1880–1840. In J. S. Becker and B. France, eds., *Folk roots, new roots: Folklore in American life,* 103–40. Lexington, MA: Museum of Our National Heritage.

LeVine, R. A. 1974. *Culture and personality: Contemporary readings.* Chicago: Aldine.

Lewicki, R. J., B. Barry, and D. M. Saunders. 2007. *Essentials of negotiation.* Boston: McGraw-Hill/Irwin.

Lewis, A. 2003. *Race in the schoolyard.* New Brunswick: Rutgers University Press.

Liebow, E. 1966. *Tally's corner: A study of Negro streetcorner men.* Boston: Little, Brown.

Lorenz, E. N. 1993. *The essence of chaos.* Seattle: University of Washington Press.

Makishima, S. 2001. *Pattern dynamics: A theory of self-organization.* Tokyo: Kodansha Scientific.

Malone, J. 1996. *Steppin' on the blues: The visible rhythms of African American dance.* Urbana: University of Illinois press.

Mayall, B. 2002. *Towards a sociology for childhood: Thinking from children's lives.* Buckingham: Open University Press.

Mead, G. H. 1999. *Play, school, and society.* Ed. M. J. Deegan. New York: Lang.

Mearnes, H. 1958. *Creative power: The education of youth in the creative arts.* New York: Dover.

Merrill-Mirsky, C. 1988. Eeny meeny pepsadeeny: Ethnicity and gender in children's musical play. Ph.D. diss., University of California.

Morris, D. 1977. *Manwatching: A field guide to human behavior.* New York: Abrams.

Nealon, J. T., and C. T. Irr. 2002. *Rethinking the Frankfurt School: Alternative legacies of cultural critique.* Albany: State University of New York Press.

Newell, W. W. 1883/1963. *Games and songs of American children.* New York: Dover.

Olssen, M. 1999. *Michel Foucault: Materialism and education.* Westport, CT: Bergin and Garvey.

Olweus, D. 1993. Bullies on the playground: The role of victimization. In C. Hart, ed., *Children on playgrounds: Research perspective and applications*, 85–128. Albany: State University of New York Press.

Olwig, K. F., and E. Gullov. 2003. *Children's places: Cross-cultural perspectives*. London: Routledge.

Opie, I. 1993/2001. *The people in the playground*. Oxford: Oxford University Press.

Opie, I., and P. Opie. 1968. *The lore and language of school children*. Oxford: Oxford University Press.

Opie, I., and P. Opie. 1969. *Children's games in street and playground*. Oxford: Oxford University Press.

Opie, I., and P. Opie. 1988. *The singing game*. Oxford: Oxford University Press.

Paley, V. G. 1988. *Bad guys don't have birthdays: Fantasy play at four*. Chicago: University of Chicago Press.

Parker-Pope, T. 2009. The 3 R's? A fourth is crucial, too: Recess. *New York Times*, February 24.

Parrot, S. 1972. Games children play: Ethnography of a second-grade recess. In J. Spradley and D. McCordy, eds., *The cultural experience*, 207–19. Chicago: Science Research Associates.

Pellegrini, A. D. 1995. *School recess and playground behavior: Educational and developmental roles*. Albany: Sate University of New York Press.

Pellegrini, A. D. 2005. *Recess: Its role in education and development*. Mahwah, NJ: Erlbaum.

Pellegrini, A. D., and P. Blatchford. 2000. *The child at school: Interactions with peers and teachers*. London: Arnold.

Pentikainen, J. 1986. Transition rites. In U. Bianchi, ed., *Transition rites: Cosmic, social, and individual order*, 1–24. Rome: Bretschneider.

Percelay, J., M. Ivey, and S. Dweck. 1994. *Snaps: If ugliness were bricks, your mother would be a housing project*. New York: Morrow.

Piaget, J. 1962. *Play, dreams, and imitation in childhood*. New York: Norton.

Piaget, J. 1965. *The moral judgment of the child*. New York: Free Press.

Pike, K. 1954. *Language in relation to a unified theory of the structure of human behavior*. Glendale, CA: Summer Institute of Linguistics.

Pitcher, E., and E. Prelinger. 1963. *Children tell stories: An analysis of fantasy*. New York: International Universities.

Popkewitz, T. S., and M. Brennan. 1998. *Foucault's challenge: Discourse, knowledge, and power in education*. New York: Teachers College Press.

Ritchie, O. W., and M. R. Koller. 1964. *Sociology of childhood*. New York: Meredith.

Ritzer, G. 1998. *The Mcdonaldization thesis*. London: Sage.

Root-Bernstein, R., and M. Root-Bernstein. 1999. *Sparks of genius: The thirteen thinking tools of the world's most creative people*. New York: Houghton Mifflin.

Rose, D. 1975. Detachment: Continuities of sensibility among Afro-American populations of the circum-Atlantic fringe. In R. D. Abrahams and J. Szwed, eds., *Discovering Afro America*, 68–82. Leiden: Brill.

Rose, T. 1994. *Black noise: Rap music and black culture in contemporary America*. Hanover, NH: Wesleyan University Press.

Salen, Katie, and Eric Zimmerman. 2004. *Rules of play: Game design fundamentals*. Cambridge: MIT Press.

Sardar, Z., and I. Abrams. 1999. *Introducing chaos*. Cambridge: Icon.

Scheper-Hughes, N., and C. Sargent. 1998. *Small wars: The cultural politics of childhood*. Berkeley: University of California Press.

Schlosser, E. 2002. *Fast food nation: The dark side of the all-American meal*. New York: Perennial.

Schmookler, A. B. 1993. *The illusion of choice: How the market economy shapes our destiny*. Albany: State University of New York Press.

Schofield, J. W. 2007. Increasing the generalizability of qualitative research. In M. Hammersley, ed., *Educational research and evidence-based practice*. Milton Keynes: Open University Press.

Schor, J. B. 2004. *Born to buy: The commercialized child and the new consumer culture*. New York: Scribner.

Schwartzman, H. 1978. *Transformations: The anthropology of children's play*. New York: Plenum.

Schwartzman, H. 2001. *Children and anthropology: Perspectives for the twenty-first Century*. Westport, CT: Bergin and Garvey.

Scott, J. 1990. *Domination and the arts of resistance: Hidden transcripts*. New Haven: Yale University Press.

Seeger, Pete. 1955/1997. *Birds, Beasts, Bugs, and Fishes Little and Big: Animal Folk Songs*. Smithsonian Folkways.

Seligman, M. 1995. *The optimistic child*. Boston: Houghton Mifflin.

Seligman, M. 2002. *Authentic happiness: Using the new positive psychology to realize your potential for lasting fulfillment*. New York: Free Press.

Shore, B. 1996. *Culture in mind: Cognition, culture, and the problem of meaning*. Oxford: Oxford University Press.

Shulman, D., and G. Stroumsa. 1999. *Dream cultures: Explorations in the comparative history of dreaming*. New York: Oxford University Press.

Singer, D., and J. Singer. 1990. *House of make believe: Children's play and the developing imagination*. Cambridge: Harvard University Press.

Sluckin, A. 1981. *Growing up in the playground*. London: Routledge.

Smith, K. W., and D. N. Berg. 1987. *Paradoxes of group life: Understanding conflict, paralysis, and movement in group dynamics*. San Francisco: Jossey-Bass.

Stallybrass, P., and A. White. 1986. *Politics and poetics of transgression*. Ithaca: Cornell University Press.

Strauss, A. L. 1978. *Negotiations: Varieties, contexts, processes, and social order*. San Francisco: Jossey-Bass.

Stephens, R. J. 2005. Hip-hop. In M. K. Asante and A. Mazana, eds., *Encyclopedia of black studies*, 263–67. Thousand Oaks, CA: Sage.

Stewart, S. 1978. *Nonsense: Aspects of intertextuality in folklore and literature*. Baltimore: Johns Hopkins University Press.

Suomi, S. J., and H. Harlow. 1976. Monkeys without play. In J. S. Bruner, A. Jolly, and K. Sylva, eds., *Play—Its role in development and evolution*, 490–95. New York: Basic Books.

Sutton-Smith, B. 1972a. *The folkgames of children*. Austin: University of Texas Press.

Sutton-Smith, B. 1972b. Games of order and disorder. Paper presented at the meeting of the American Anthropological Association, Toronto.

Sutton-Smith, B. 1976. *Games of the Americas.* New York: Adorno.

Sutton-Smith, B. 1978. The dialectics of play. In F. Landry, and W. Oban, eds., *Physical activity and human well-being.* Miami: Symposia Specialists.

Sutton-Smith, B. 1981a. *The folkstories of children.* Philadelphia: University of Pennsylvania Press.

Sutton-Smith, B. 1981b. *A history of children's play: The New Zealand playground, 1840–1950.* Philadelphia: University of Pennsylvania Press.

Sutton-Smith, B. 1989. Models of power. In R. Bolton, ed., *The content of culture-constants and variants: Studies in honor of John M. Roberts,* 3–18. New Haven, CT: Human Relations Area Files Press.

Sutton-Smith, B. 1997. *The ambiguity of play.* Cambridge: Harvard University Press.

Sutton-Smith, B., J. Mechling, J. T. Johnson, and F. McMahon. 1995. *Children's folklore: A source book.* Logan: Utah State University Press.

Swartz, D. 1997. *Culture and power: The sociology of Pierre Bourdieu.* Chicago: University of Chicago Press.

Tannen, D. 2007. *Talking voices: Repetition, dialogue, and imagery in conversational discourse.* Cambridge: Cambridge University Press.

Thompson, R. F. 1975. An introduction to transatlantic black art history: Remarks in anticipation of a coming golden age of Afro-Americana. In R. D. Abrahams and J. Szwed, eds., *Discovering Afro-America,* 58–67. Leiden: Brill.

Thorne, B. 1993. *Gender play: Girls and boys at school.* New Brunswick: Rutgers University Press.

Toop, D. 1984/1991. *Rap attack 2: African rap to global hip-hop.* London: Serpent's Tail.

Turner, V. 1982. *From ritual to theatre: The human seriousness of play.* New York: Performing Arts Journal Press.

Turner, V. 1987. Betwixt and between. The liminal period in rites of passage. In L. C. Mahdi, S. Foster, and M. Little, eds. *Betwixt and between: Patterns of masculine and feminine initiation,* 3–22. La Salle, IL: Open Court.

Tylor, E. B. 1971. The history of games. In E. M. Avedon and B. Sutton-Smith, eds., *The study of games,* 63–76. New York: Wiley.

Vanderbilt, T. 1998. *The sneaker book: Anatomy of an industry and an icon.* New York: New Press.

van Gennep, A. 1960. *The rites of passage.* Trans. M. B. Vizedom and G. L. Caffee. Chicago: University of Chicago Press.

Vygotsky, L. S. 1978. *Mind in society: The development of higher psychological processes.* Ed. M. Cole. Cambridge: Harvard University Press.

Wallace, A. F. C. 1961. *Culture and personality.* New York: Random House.

Weis, L. 1988. *Class, race, and gender in American education.* Albany: State University of New York Press.

West, C. 2001. *Race matters.* Boston: Beacon.

West, C. 2004. *Democracy matters: Winning the fight against imperialism.* New York: Penguin.

Whiting, B. B. 1963. *Six cultures: Studies of child rearing.* New York: Wiley.

Whiting, B. B., and C. P. Edwards. 1988. *Children of different worlds: The formation of social behavior.* Cambridge: Harvard University Press.

Whitten, N. E., Jr., and J. Szwed, eds. 1970. *Afro-American anthropology: Contemporary perspectives*. New York: Free Press.

Whyte, W. F. 1943. *Street corner society: The social structure of an Italian slum*. Chicago: University of Chicago Press.

Wiggershaus, R. W. 1994. *The Frankfurt school: Its history, theories, and political significance*. Trans. M. Robertson. Cambridge: MIT Press.

Williams, R. 1976. *Keywords: A vocabulary of culture and society*. New York: Oxford University Press.

Willie, C. V. 1983. *Race, ethnicity, and socioeconomic status: A theoretical analysis of their interrelationship*. Bayside, NY: General Hall.

Willie, C. V., and J. Beker. 1973. *Race mixing in the public schools*. New York: Praeger.

Willis, P. 1977. *Learning to labor: How working class kids get working class jobs*. New York: Columbia University Press.

Willis, P. 1990. *Common culture: Symbolic work at play in the everyday cultures of the young*. Boulder, CO: Westview.

Winner, E., and H. Gardner. 1979. *Fact, fiction, and fantasy in childhood*. San Francisco: Jossey-Bass.

Winnicott, D. W. 1971. *Playing and reality*. London: Tavistock.

Young, F. W. 1965. *Initiation ceremonies: A cross-cultural study of status dramatization*. Indianapolis: Bobbs-Merrill.

INDEX